THE
ALCOHOLICIRONMAN

THE
ALCOHOLICIRONMAN
JOHN TOTH

A MEMOIR

TATE PUBLISHING & *Enterprises*

Published by Tate Publishing & Enterprises, LLC
127 E. Trade Center Terrace | Mustang, Oklahoma 73064 USA
1.888.361.9473 | www.tatepublishing.com

Tate Publishing is committed to excellence in the publishing industry. The company reflects the philosophy established by the founders, based on Psalm 68:11,
"The Lord gave the word and great was the company of those who published it."

Book design copyright © 2011 by Tate Publishing, LLC. All rights reserved.
Cover design by Kenna Davis
Interior design by Joel Uber

Published in the United States of America

ISBN: 978-1-61346-147-1
Biography & Autobiography: Personal Memoirs
11.07.25

To my wife, Jennifer, without whose constant love and support none of this would have been possible.

Amount of times I told myself I couldn't do this = 1,972
Amount of diets I quit = 22
Amount of self doubting thoughts I had = 119,227
Amount of books I read to prepare for this event = 11
Amount of times I didn't believe I could do it = 1,472
Amount of times I told my wife that I quit = 15
Amount of times that I actually quit = 10,000
Amount of times I got back up and kept going = 10,001

TABLE OF CONTENTS

I Can't Run?

Wow, how did we get here? It's August 14, 2009. Two days ago, I signed up for what most people would consider physical suicide, the 2010 Ironman in Lake Placid, New York. The word *Ironman* has such an aura about it. We picture tough, semi-crazed athletes going distances the human body wasn't designed to go. Most of us have probably seen an Ironman on ABC's *Wide World of Sports* at some point. I know I did—those finely tuned athletes trudging their way across the Hawaii lava fields. It looked insane. For every person you saw smiling, there were three people behind him who were trying to keep their bodies from hitting the pavement. How could the human body endure a 2.4-mile swim and a 112-mile bike ride, followed by a full marathon? Impossible! For those of you counting at home, the marathon is 26.2 miles, bringing the total race distance to 140.6 miles in one day.

Ouch!

For some reason, the thought of an Ironman had always fascinated me. I don't know why. I am in no way an endurance athlete; in fact, I'm just the opposite. Although I have proven in my life to have tremendous willpower on some things, I have absolutely no willpower on others, as you will see. I was a pretty athletic kid growing up but lacked the mental competitiveness to care. My body had a lot of talent, but my mind didn't. I could hit a baseball hard and far. I could throw 78 mph when I was thirteen and with a decent wind at my back, I can hit a three iron 250 yards. My problem with all those things was my head.

So now I sit here, thirty-nine years old, getting ready to start one of the most difficult and potentially rewarding journeys of my life. I thought it would be interesting to document my journey along the way. My goal is to be as open and honest as I can through the good and bad. There will be plenty of both.

Before we begin on this self-inflicted roller coaster of mine, I think it's important to tell you how I got here.

Rewind to 2002. I was in the process of trying to figure out what I wanted to do with my life. After a failed attempt at rock stardom (thanks, Nirvana), I entered what some people call the real world. I had a career or what I guess most people would call a job. I had no idea what I wanted to do. I had a lot of things that I wanted to do, but they don't usually pay people for lying on a beach or singing in bars. For the record, I still don't know what I want to do.

My father was a police officer in the City of Brotherly Love. One of my dad's goals in life was to make sure that I didn't become a cop. He would tell me stories that were probably inappropriate for a child to hear, but I knew what he was trying to do. And it worked. Enough scary stories later, I chose not to enter that career path. In all fairness, my father was a much tougher guy than I am. I'm not sure if it was because I spent most of my life growing up with my mother or he was just hardened by his own tough childhood, but I don't want to pretend that I could step in any cop's shoes and do his job.

With all of that being said, I had thoughts here and there about joining the Pennsylvania State Police. I still had some kind of desire to do that kind of work, and while the "staties" were tough-looking dudes, it was a less dangerous job than a major city cop. I had applied a few times and just never showed up for the test. I guess when *Cold Case Files* went off the air in the summer, I lost my enthusiasm.

After being in the professional world for a few years, I decided I hated it. I hated the games, the nonsense. I hated that there were people in jobs because they knew people. And I especially hated that no one cared about anyone or anything except making a dollar. I've seen all kinds of people laid off, fired, and let go when the company was making money. I hated it. For the record, I still hate that part of it.

So I did what any red-blooded American would do, I decided to join the FBI.

Yeah, it was a bit out of left field for my family as well. My wife, not wanting to discourage me, said it was okay. I think she assumed I wouldn't get all the way to the end of their rigorous hiring process. One of the biggest problems of working for the FBI is that they can relocate you anywhere in the world. We already had a house and kids; my wife had a teaching job that she worked really hard to get. It wouldn't be easy, but I was determined.

So I took the test. I have to say that the test was no joke. The entire special agent selection process is designed to "weed out the suckers." And that it does.

I had taken the written test and passed, which started a waterfall of events that happened over the next twelve months. From person-to-person interviews to information sessions to a phase-two interview that consisted of a written test and a three-agent panel interviewing me, I went through it all. It was a real study in psychology and bureaucracy at its best.

One of biggest requirements to get into the FBI was that you take a physical test. Now, when I first heard this, I thought it was going to be something like the test that you take in grade school, fifty sit-ups and twenty pushups. Run without your pants falling down, pass! Unfortunately, this is not how the FBI works. I can honestly say from all the research I did, the FBI had one of the hardest physical standards I had seen. They expected people to already be in shape when they got to Quantico, unlike the military, where they will whip you into shape during training.

The test did consist of pushups and sit-ups, but it also included pull ups (not easy for a 225-pound man) and a timed 1.5-mile run. Each of these was hard. It wasn't like you did fifteen pushups. You were scored on how many you could do. I remember at the time, my goal was fifty pushups. One of the reasons I needed to do so many pushups was because I already knew that I was going to get clobbered in the run. The maximum time for the 1.5-mile run was twelve minutes. That's right, eight-minute miles. So I needed to get the highest score in other things to make up for my sluggish running.

One key part I have failed to mention thus far was that I was starting to struggle with a drinking problem that I had been nursing for years. Alcoholism was in my family. Both my grandfather and father had it. My father had been sober for about twenty-five years when my struggles began. I was a textbook case of a functional alcoholic—paid my mortgage, never got fired from a job, and didn't crash my car into any poles. But I was physically, emotionally, and spiritually bankrupt. Toward the end of my drinking, I hated life. I was often disappointed when I actually woke up in the morning that I was still alive. It's difficult to explain unless you have gone through it.

Here I was, a healthy man with a wife, kids, and a house in the suburbs, and I was miserable. Part of the problem was that I was my own worst judge and jury and beat myself up senselessly for everything, especially for not appreciating what I had.

Restless, irritable, discontented, depressed, suicidal, and homicidal; for any of you who have struggled with alcoholism, these words will sound familiar. They described me to a T. I was a mess and slowly falling apart. I was physically deteriorating and didn't even care. But if I wanted to get into the FBI, I would have to make some changes.

I knew that on paper, I was a good candidate for the feds. I had a management degree and an MS in information science. Having already decided that I was going to get invited to Quantico, I decided that it was time to start training. For a person that had so little self-control over alcohol, I have amazing self-control when I need it.

So I started exercising again. I had always been what I termed "an exerciser." I was always fiddling around with the weights but never seriously. I would go through periods of time where I would really be into it and then phase out or be too hung over to care. One of the things that the thought of Quantico did was give me this impending event that I thought was going to happen. My theory was that if I was going to quit my job, go away for four months, and mess up my home life, I better pass the first time!

Even though I was in fair shape, most of my exercise for the past fifteen years had been weight lifting. I wasn't even a bit aerobically fit. As a kid, I played baseball and hockey, neither of which requires you to run for long periods of time.

So there I was at the local high school track with my sneakers all laced up, ready to tear it up. I was going to be in the FBI and show everyone my badge and gun. I was going to carry my gun on the plane with me wherever I went. I was going to be a big shot. I was going to set the record for the fastest mile ever run.

I made it about a hundred yards when I first realized what a disaster I was. I can't remember exactly, but I think I made it about one-half to two-thirds around the track before I had to stop, with my hands on my knees, doubled over in pain. Not only could I not breathe but also my legs had atrophied so much from drinking and not doing anything physical that my legs and feet were killing me. I was dying.

Being an extremely hardheaded German/Hungarian, I, of course, kept trying. I tried and tried and failed and failed. I would make myself run through the pain and suffer the whole time. First, I thought it was the shoes, and then I thought it was my feet, and then I thought it was because I was too big; then it was because I wasn't built right.

Turns out it was the drinking. Pumping almost three-quarters of a bottle of vodka into your body each night apparently doesn't help your body perform at its best. Who knew? I'm really not the sharpest tool in the shed.

This process went on for almost two years. From start to finish, that's about how long the whole FBI process takes. A lot of it is because they are a bureaucracy, and a lot of it is how fast you could research the last thirty years of your life. When you join the federal government in a position that could potentially give you top-secret clearance, they tend to want to know what you've been involved in during your entire life. The application itself was their own best rendition of *War and Peace*. Nevertheless, this went on for two years, me trying to exercise and then giving up and then feeling bad and starting again. I kept coming up with excuse after excuse. First it was, "Well, I'll wait until 120 days before Quantico starts, and then I'll quit drinking and really exercise hard." Then it was ninety, then sixty. You get the picture.

In between all of these nonsensical arguments I used to have with myself, I would often have moments that only another true alcoholic could understand. I used to go down to Wildwood, New Jersey, in the summer and drink all night. Then I would make myself get up at 6:00 a.m. and run on the beach. In my mind, if the drinking was keeping me from running in the morning, then I would have to admit that I had a problem. It was easier to just suffer for an hour running than it was to admit that I had a problem. So there I was, 225 pounds of slop, running down the beach with my shirt off, absolutely sweating my butt off. I was dying. Half of the people on the beach were looking at me. More than likely, they could smell the alcohol pouring out of my body. But I kept running. I was going to be in the FBI.

Needless to say, that strategy didn't work. I kept trying to run, and I kept failing. I would have big highs, where I thought I was going to be the next director of the FBI, to big lows, where I couldn't believe anyone would hire me for anything.

The thing that most people don't realize about alcoholism is that it is a disease of feelings and emotions. The drinking is only the part you see on the outside. It's how we feel and perceive things that makes us drink ourselves to oblivion. I used to get irritated at the notion that alcoholism was a disease. It wasn't cancer or AIDS. But it killed just as many people, either directly or indirectly. It took me a long time to realize that it is a mental disease, just like anorexia or masochism.

Day after day, it was more of the same thing. I would wake up in the morning and promise myself I wasn't going to drink. Then by 5:00 p.m., I was convincing myself that I deserved it. I would switch from wine to vodka to Scotch and back again. I had aspirations of becoming a wine connoisseur, only to end up drinking wine out of a box. Each day, I would promise myself, and each day, I would fail. Each week, I would start a new exercise routine, and by Tuesday, I would quit. I went through this process for years.

Then it happened. In reality, it was a much longer event than one night, but it was the night that changed my life. I had known that I had a drinking problem for a long time. I truly just didn't care. I thought I was going to fool the FBI and everyone else. I was not opposed to cleaning myself up because I hated the way that I felt—empty, lonely, suicidal.

My cousin Tom and I spent a lot of time together in the years before I got sober. Our parents, his mom and my mom, were sisters and owned a shore property together. So we would go down there a lot and have our parents watch the kids, and we would go out drinking til all hours of the night.

Tom also had season tickets to the Philadelphia Eagles games. What this entailed was him driving up to my house and picking me up at 7:00 a.m. (for 1:00 p.m. games) and going back to his house. We would sit at his kitchen table and eat some breakfast sandwiches and wash them down with shots of Jameson. After that and a few beers, we would walk over to the local sports bar Chickie's and Pete's and get on the big green Eagles bus. This was a private bus that took about thirty lunatics down to the Eagles games. For $30 bucks, it was all you could eat and drink. It was heaven—beer, food, and someone else was driving. It didn't get any better. I loved it. They could have let me sit there until the end of time and I would have been happy. When it was all over, I walked to the train station, and my wife would pick me up and bring me home.

This Sunday was like any other Sunday during football season, sitting in Tom's kitchen eating pork roll and cheese sandwiches drinking Jameson like it was keeping me alive. I drank my fair share the rest of the day too but nothing out of the ordinary. It was the Cowboys versus the Eagles. It was a rainy, cold, miserable afternoon in December. It was 2004 the year the Eagles went to the Super Bowl, and it was pretty late in the season, so it was an important game. The Eagles ended up winning in the fourth quarter thirteen to seven, but it wasn't pretty. We left the game in the middle of the fourth quarter to go sit in the warm, dry bus. From there, we watched on the TV as the birds won, and we drank away the afternoon.

When the game was over, I remember sitting there drinking beers as fast as I could. I wanted to make sure I had a buzz on for the train ride home. I remember looking at the top of the can that was only centimeters away from my eyes as I poured the beer down my throat, thinking, *I can't even taste this.* Then I opened another and did the same thing. I probably drank about four beers in a matter of minutes. Then I poured two into a red Solo cup as the bus was leaving and started walking to the train station. I remember walking because I couldn't. A ten-foot straight line ended up being a forty-five-foot zigzag walk. I was all over the place. I think I was stumbling so much that I actually had to sit down for a bit. Eventually, I made my way to the train. Like any good alcoholic, I had a bottle of water and a sandwich stashed in my jacket. Most alcoholics don't like to imbibe anything that's not alcohol. I was the opposite; I drank water and ate so I could keep drinking. Once I had a bottle of water and a sandwich in me, I felt better, probably still really drunk, but better.

As usual, I got off the train, and the wife picked me up, our usual Sunday football game routine. The difference was that when I got home, I started drinking like I did every night after work. Being a functional alcoholic, I made work every day. But when I came home at six o'clock, I immediately poured myself a martini, a big martini. Not one, three. It came out to about three-quarters of a bottle. That was on the weeknights. Week-ends were usually more.

Much like my dreams of becoming a wine connoisseur, I transferred those skills into other areas. I started off with vodka like Stoli and Grey Goose and ended up buying half gallons of Gilby's for $15.

On this particular Sunday, I got home from the game and plopped on the couch. It was sometime around dinnertime. That's when I started drinking martinis. Funny thing about my Martinis was that I didn't even own any vermouth, and if I had olives to put in them, I was lucky. Nevertheless, I drank them as if they were my first drink of the day. So on top of all the Whiskey I had earlier and all of the beer, I was now drinking vodka, a lot of it.

The rest of the night was uneventful. Like most functional alcoholics, I didn't miss work because of drinking. But this Monday was different. I woke up not feeling right. I felt like I had been hit by a truck. I had had hangovers before, but this was one for the ages. I decided that a shower, some coffee, and something greasy would get me going. I made it to work and immediately knew something was wrong. I didn't feel right at all. I knew I was hung over, but this was something different—something worse, way worse.

I got to work and started looking up things on the Internet, because everyone knows that self-diagnosis is the best way to go.

Leave it to me to look up alcohol poisoning on the Internet. I read all of the symptoms and had them all. After about forty-five minutes, I was in such bad shape that I left work and went home to an empty house. I again started looking up alcohol poisoning and really started scaring myself. One of the things that people don't realize about alcohol is that it warps your mind and your thinking. I was irrational, delusional, and full of fear. I was scared to death and paranoid out of my mind. When you're drinking, you don't realize that it's the alcohol.

So now I was home, alone, freaking out. Half of it was because I was going through alcohol poisoning and the other half because I was having a full-blown panic attack. And then it began, the pacing. What was I going to do? It was four days before Christmas, and I was going to ruin everyone's holiday because they were going to have to come see me in the hospital or worse, a funeral parlor. I started freaking out, pacing incessantly. I was slowing wearing a triangular path into my carpet by pacing from my bathroom to the kitchen to the front door.

Should I call my father who had been sober for twenty-five years? No, that's too embarrassing. Should I just drive myself to the hospital? No, that's too embarrassing. Should I call my wife at work? No way. So I paced. I paced, and I paced. This went on for two hours. At one point, I actually pulled out the phone book and looked up rehabs. I dialed an 800 number that to this day I wish I still had because I would call them and tell them off. A woman answered. She was clearly not in recovery nor did she care about mine; she just wanted to get me to her rehab in Florida. I'm guessing she got commission. So she asked me a few questions and then told me to get on a plane.

A plane? That was too much for me. I told her I would call her back later and resumed my pacing. After a few hours, I got back to the bathroom and stopped. I looked into the mirror and had one of those experiences that only God can give you. I looked in the mirror. All I could think about was my family, my wife, my kids, my parents; it all flashed before me. I looked into that mirror and said with all my heart and soul, "God, if you get me out of this, I promise I will never take another sip of anything as long as I live."

I paced a couple more times and then went to the bedroom. For those of you that have been through this, you realize how impossible it is to fall asleep when you're going through withdrawal. Through the grace of God, I fell asleep. That was my first miracle.

A couple hours later, my wife came home from work. She was greeted by a mess of a man. She no sooner walked in the door and sent the kids upstairs than she had me draped over her crying my eyes out telling her I needed help. I was done. I completely surrendered. Finally.

Being the wonderful spouse that she is, she said, "Okay, then we'll get you help."

The next day, I planned what I was going to do. I had made a promise to that mirror and had intended to keep it. But for the next couple of days, I needed to wean myself off of the booze. So on Tuesday night, I think I had one martini and one glass of wine. Then on Wednesday, I had one glass of wine. On Thursday, I made my way to a twelve-step group around the corner from my house. It was a small local church, and there were only about seven people in the room.

There was a man at the front of the room who seemed to be running the show.

The man said, "Is this anyone's first time here?"

I raised my hand and said, "My name is John, and I'm an alcoholic".

They said welcome. Then he said, "Is this anyone's first time at this meeting?"

I raised my hand and said, "My name is John, and I'm an alcoholic."

They said welcome. Then he said, "Is there anyone here with less than ninety days of sobriety?"

I raised my hand and said, "My name is John, and I'm an alcoholic."

Thus began my journey of recovery.

YEAR ONE

Going from the self-appointed head of the FBI to crying on my wife's shoulder begging for help was somewhat overwhelming. The journey of an alcoholic is just that, a journey. Most people think we are just idiots who like to drink too much. In most cases, that's not really true. In most cases, we are childish, insecure, and full of fear. We drink because we are uncomfortable in our own skin. A lot of people don't understand because they think we are choosing to drink. The reality is that we have to drink in order to feel okay with ourselves. That's what people who aren't alcoholics don't understand.

The first six months to a year were a complete blur. Between going to as many 12-step meetings as I could make and white knuckling it the rest of the time, I was exhausted. You would think that with all of that going on, that year would just fly by. It didn't. In fact, it was just the opposite. That was the longest year of my life.

When you quit drinking, it is a complete change of lifestyle. You don't do the same things that you used to do. You don't behave the same way, and you don't have the same crutch that has gotten you through all of those uncomfortable situations.

Part of me hates to say that because I think it scares people who are thinking about getting sober. They think they are going to lose all their friends and not have any fun anymore. That's not true at all. But you do have to make some changes. I hate to use the term reborn, but it is truly a rebirth. You take baby steps but not until you are ready. You have to do things that you had never done sober before, like going to a family party or a holiday party at work. You go through your first Christmas and New Year's and Fourth of July, all for the first time sober since you were a kid. That first year was tough.

For those of you who don't know that much about alcoholism, I got sober in December. The first question I said to someone was, "What am I going to do next summer?" Not Christmas or New Year's, but next summer. That's how twisted our thinking can get at times.

So I started my journey to sobriety by raising my hand at that meeting three times in a row and admitting defeat. I was ready. It was my time.

After the meeting, a couple of guys sat down with me. Had you asked me to sit with these guys even three days before, I would have laughed at you. Or more than likely, I would have listened, pretended I cared, and went home and started drinking.

This time was different, I was begging for their help. I was not going to orphan my kid. This was not how it was going to happen.

So they sat down with me, Craig and Bob. I told them my story for about ten minutes.

When I was done talking, Bob looked at me with a smile on his face and said, "John, you never have to feel this way again."

I sucked that up. I felt like I had been hit by a fire truck followed by a steamroller. But it wasn't just the withdrawal and hangover. I knew what he meant. I was physically, emotionally, and spiritually bankrupt. I had reached my own personal bottom and was ready. I was all ears. Willingness is half the battle they say, and man, was I willing.

So we talked for about an hour. They told me their stories, and I told them mine. In typical fashion, I tried to get by with a half-cocked scheme to not really have to go to meetings and talk to anyone. For at least three months before I got sober, I was playing around on the Internet and going to online 12-step meetings. I thought they were great because I could sit and watch and never have to say anything. It's a fairly long process to figure out and admit that one has a problem. It's embarrassing, and embarrassment is my number one fear. With the online meetings, I could just sit there and do some research without anyone seeing or hearing me. More than likely, I even used a fake name. I can't remember!

One of the first things I said to Bob was, "I've been going to some online meetings."

He said, "I've never been to one. Sounds okay, but you need to go to some meetings in person."

Being the right time and the right place, I decided to listen to him, even though I didn't want to. Every part of my body didn't want to, but my way got me a seat in this room. He gave me a book of local places that had meetings all hours of the day and night. I had no excuse. Even worse, he told me I had to do ninety meetings in ninety days. Ouch! But I hurt so bad, I would have gone naked if they told me to. I got my stack of literature, shook both of their hands, and went on my way.

When I got home that night, my wife was, of course, curious to see how I was. She had seen me quit drinking for a few days or weeks a thousand times, so she was a bit skeptical. Nevertheless, I came home and told her about the whole thing. I ended the whole conversation with, "Ninety meetings in ninety days."

"Ninety meetings in ninety days?" she said. But she never discouraged me. She supported me the whole time. Luckily for both of us, I have always been a pretty considerate person most of my life. I was the kid that came in at 3:00 a.m. and no one ever heard me. That's probably why I got away with so much. Because of this, I tried to squeeze in as many meetings in as I could at lunch and before work so that I wouldn't completely disrupt everyone's life. I got hooked up with a group right around the corner from my house that had a 7:00 a.m. meeting every day. I was there at 7:00 a.m. Saturday and Sunday and home with doughnuts and coffee for the family before they woke up. It still wasn't easy, but I knew if I didn't do it, I was sunk.

Quitting drinking for ninety days really isn't that hard. Most of us alcoholics have done periods of time like that in our drinking careers. It's staying stopped that's the hard part. When you go to ninety meetings in ninety days, you are constantly surrounded by the right people. You hear a combination of hope and sorrow that keep you going. For me, I think the harder part was the second ninety days. This is when you start feeling a bit better mentally and physically. You start hearing some things and thinking that the guy next to you is way worse than you. This is where the disease starts playing games with your head. It tells you that you can drink. That you just had a bad stretch. They often say about alcoholism that it is the only disease that tells yourself you don't have it. And it's true. It is constantly trying to get you back. If you don't pay attention, it does. That's why so many people die from this disease.

I remember sitting in a meeting early on and thinking to myself, *Is this for me? They all seem way worse than me.* But for some reason, I kept going back week after week, my biggest struggles coming on the weekend. That's when the family parties, football games, and free time were.

I had spent a fair amount of time in the preceding years looking to fill that proverbial hole in the doughnut inside me. Something was missing, and I didn't know what. I felt empty inside. I tried yoga, meditation, exercise. You name it, I tried it. I bought every book you could think of, from *The Power of Positive Thinking* by Norman Vincent Peal to the Bible to books on Buddhism. Tony Robbins even has a place on my shelf. I looked and I looked, but I couldn't find it. The most extensive research I had done was looking at the bottom of an empty bottle, constantly looking for the answer.

Here I was in a room full of people who had something. I wanted it.

I clearly remember sitting there saying to myself, "These people have something that I want." They had a look on their face. They looked happy. They looked like they were living life instead of sitting on the sidelines watching it. Right then, I thought to myself, *I'm going to give this a try and see how I feel in a year.* To me, that was as long a commitment I was willing to make. Forever sounded long, and one day at time just didn't work for me. I was aiming for a year.

Luckily for me, I have been a fairly good listener most of my life—not because I'm an angel, mostly because of fear. Fear of getting in trouble, I suppose, helped me along the way. I was also really good at talking my way out of things or seeing trouble before it got there. Fortunately for me, this is one of the best qualities you can have in getting sober. You have to be teachable, and you have to follow the examples of those before you who have done it.

I got sober in December. Two weeks later, I had tickets to the Philadelphia Eagles NFC Championship game in Philly. I didn't go. They told me stay away from "people, places, and things." So I did. I didn't want to get drunk. They told me that I needed to go to ninety meetings in ninety days. I did. I didn't miss a single one. They told me to get a sponsor. I did, a little, gay, black man. We had absolutely nothing in common, but we were both drunks. I spent all of my free time with him. He singlehandedly carried me through my first year. My first New Year's, they told me I should lay low. I did. I stayed home. I was willing to do whatever it took to stay sober; I was in bed at 10:00 p.m.

I had many nights that I had to white-knuckle myself through, but I didn't always have to do it alone. There were other guys who were doing the same thing. We hung out together. We went on golfing trips together. We smoked cigarettes and drank coffee. We watched football games together. And if one of us was in a rough patch, he called the other ones. Every day brought a new challenge, and every day we had to live life. It wasn't going to stop just for us.

Over the year, one of the things that I found the most fascinating is how little regular people really know about alcoholics. They just think we are irresponsible drunks who make bad decisions and ruin our own lives. While there may certainly be an element of that in some cases, it's not really that simple. This is an emotional disease. Drinking is the tip of the iceberg. Drinking is a disease of feelings and emotions, even for the tough guys. Drinking is about how we feel inside and our inability to deal with reality.

As an outsider, you can look at two people getting sober. One can be a millionaire, and one can be a streetwalker. To a non-alcoholic, the millionaire has a better chance of getting sober and should have an easier time. This is absolutely not true. They go through the same things. They go through the fear, the uncertainly, the loneliness, the restlessness, the anger, the irritability, the discontentment. Sure, one may pay their rent easier than the other and one may have fewer worries than the other, but if they are both alcoholics, they face the same journey.

A lot of alcoholic programs don't believe in telling you whether or not you are an alcoholic. They feel that only you can tell. I have gone back and forth on this idea for some time. It took me a while to understand it, but when I finally did, I got it. I knew what they meant. For me, it was simply getting to a place in my life where I was ready to turn it around. It was that simple to me. If you're not ready to admit to yourself and your Creator that you have a problem, you have very little chance of cleaning up.

Over time, I have started to disagree with that statement to some extent. I still agree with that statement as a whole but feel that as a sober person we are missing out on an opportunity to educate people about the reality of alcoholism and drug addiction. I think there are some telltale warning signs that people may have a problem, signs that I didn't know until I got sober. Forget all of the obvious things like DUIs, amount consumed, and relationships wrecked. I'm talking about the real heart of the alcoholic problem.

Here is alcoholism in a nutshell:

Restless
Irritable
Discontent
Hungry
Angry
Lonely
Tired
Self-Pity
Self-Loathing
Fear
Resentment

It's not about drinking too much; it's about thinking too much. I imagine it's much like being shot. You can guess what it feels like to be shot but can only really know if you yourself have been shot. That is one of the lures of a twelve-step program. You are talking to people who know exactly how you feel. They're not sympathizing with you; they're empathizing with you.

About six months into my sobriety, I invited my dad out to dinner. I hadn't told him yet that I had quit. Because I didn't live with him, he didn't really know that I had a problem. The reason for the dinner was to tell him that I had gotten sober. This is how crazy we can be. I didn't tell my own father, who had been sober for around twenty-five years, that I had been sober for six months. Six months!

Why? While I have several reasons for this; I guess the biggest one was fear. Not fear that he would yell at me or be disappointed but fear that I would never be able to go back out and drink again once I told him. Once he knew, I was done for. The fear and embarrassment would have crippled me. In the end, I still would have drunk, but I would have spent a lot of time hiding it from him. I wanted to make sure I was serious about this before I brought that on myself. Six months seemed like a good time.

I had called him up the night before and asked him to go to dinner. I wouldn't tell him what it was for. I could tell by his voice he was nervous that something was up. He kept asking me if everything was all right. I kept telling him yes. So we met at a Bertucci's near my work. We sat down and looked at our menus for a minute, and then he asked the golden question, "What's up?"

I reached into my pocket and pulled out a little coin that I had gotten from my twelve-step group that said, "6 months," and slid it across the table and didn't say anything. He looked at it with so much awe and surprise, you would have thought he was sitting across from Mickey Mantle. He said one word, "You?"

We spent the next hour and a half telling each other our stories. I cried once or twice, and he listened. It felt great to share it with him, even though I was scared to death.

About halfway through dinner, he looked up at me and said, "You know, putting down the drink is the easiest part. Living sober is the hard part."

Dinner had been going so well up to that point. Now I wanted to reach across the table and strangle him. How could he say that? How could he tell me that the last six months of my life were easy? Had he lost his mind? The old man's gone batty! I would later find out that that was the most honest thing anyone had ever said to me.

We had a great night together. When it was all done, we hugged, told each other we loved each other, and went our separate ways.

Through it all, I managed to stay sober that first year. I got a lot of help from my sponsor, my dad, the man upstairs, and a whole bunch of friends. I don't know why I was able to get it that year and other people didn't. I would constantly hear stories about people dying or relapsing. But even that didn't always scare me. I would think to myself, *They are way worse than me; that won't happen to me.*

Having a year under my belt, I had kept the promise that I had made to myself. Now what would I do? For me, I decided that I liked the way I felt. Actually, I hated the way I felt but was clear enough to know the direction I needed to head in. When you go to a twelve-step meeting, there are three kinds of people. There are the people who have been sober for a long time. In most cases, they have a look on their face that is indescribable. They just look like they have it. I don't know what it is, but they have it—serenity, contentment, and happiness. You can tell the ones that have it just by looking at them. My father has it. His friends had it; I wanted it. Then there are those that are the exact opposite. Usually, people that are brand new and still beat up. They fight everyone and everything and most wind up getting drunk. They use the twelve-step meetings as a revolving door where they can come in for a few days or months to clean up, only to go back out again and start all over. Then there are the rest of us. We fall somewhere in between. We want what the old-timers have but still have the brain of the newcomers. It is here that I have spent most of my time, trying to learn which side I belong on.

I heard a quote once that gave me the motivation I needed to try to get what the old-timers had. I think it's why the Ironman is so symbolic and so similar to sobriety for me. "Just keep putting one foot in front of the other; with every step, you are further from the starting line and closer to the finish line." That hit me hard. I really understood that. Just keep putting one foot in front of the other. Not only did it make sense athletically, but also it made total sense for my sobriety. My version was something like this, "Sobriety is an uphill walk; if you stop walking, you will roll back down the hill fast." To me, every step I took, every success, every failure, were all steps forward. As long as I kept moving and kept trying, I was on the right path.

Getting Healthy

Now that I was putting one foot in front of the other, I decided it was time to get healthy. I had been sober for about a year. I had smoked cigarettes the first year just to get me through. My intention was always to quit after a year. When the year came up and I decided to stay sober, I had a talk with myself. I needed to be healthy for myself and my family. Getting fat and smoking wasn't helping anyone.

I used to live with my friend Jaime. We had a tiny apartment in Trevose, Pennsylvania. I think Jaime and I are separated in age by a few days. We both used to lift weights; we both liked to mountain bike. We both liked to drink. It's funny how life works sometimes really. I remember when we were younger and Jaime would come home from college, he could drink the whole bar under the table. He was actually smaller than me but could put away booze like no one I had ever seen. I was sure at the time he was destined to be a drunk.

It wasn't until years later that he and I moved in together. We had both been out of college for a year or two, and we didn't want to live with our parents. It was a good arrangement for both of us. We had a lot in common. We moved all of our stuff in and capped it off with a brand new "bachelor dining room set," three hundred pounds of Olympic weights and an Olympic bench! What more could two bachelors need?

He and I used to lift weights in our "dining room" almost every night. I can remember lifting weights and then wanting to have some beers when I was done. That seemed totally normal to me. Jaime didn't usually want to. I used to get kind of annoyed at him because I thought he was this big partier, but he would decline almost every time. Drinking after exercise is not a normal activity for those of you keeping score at home. For some reason, that never occurred to me.

Having been sober for over a year now, I decided that I needed something to keep me occupied. The thought of a marathon was completely out of the question. I hated to run, but I needed something. Simply lifting weights here and there wasn't doing it for me. I think there was a large part of me that needed to equate my sobriety with something. I think another part of me needed to get over the fact that I couldn't make it around the track once when I was training for the FBI. That's a quarter mile, 1,320 feet. Anytime I ran any amount of consecutive distance in a row, I was dying. With every step and every breath, I thought I was going to have a heart attack.

I'm not sure what the final reason was that made me decide on doing it, but I decided to sign up for a race. Years before, I was in a public speaking class in graduate school. One night, the professor had us all stand up and give an impromptu three-minute speech. I stood up and told some random story about me finding a $1,500 guitar in a pawnshop for $150 bucks. Nothing fantastic.

A guy in my class got up and told a story about running a marathon. He was as average as you could get—not a jock, not athletic-looking, none of the above. But what he said stuck with me for years after that.

He said, "I ran a marathon. I'm not a runner, but I decided to try it. I trained for it for six months and ran in xyz marathon. *Anyone* can do it, if they train for it." I don't know why I believed him or why that stuck with me all those years, but it did. I knew that what he said was true. Even when I was still a drunk, I knew that if I put the time into things, I could accomplish them. The problem with being a drunk is that you don't put the time in. I quit almost everything I have ever started.

So I called up a woman I worked with. I had heard at a sales meeting that she had done a marathon. I called her and asked her a hundred different questions about how she did it. I asked her everything from diet to training to shoes. You name it, I asked it. One of the good qualities that I have is that I have never been afraid to ask questions. This is one of the greatest assets I have been blessed with and something I am truly grateful for. Rabbi Harold Kushner once said, "Man's greatest sin is the arrogance of self-sufficiency." The most important thing that she told me was to sign up for the race. This was a big deal for me. I can be very brave about some things and an absolute coward about others. After all, I didn't want to tell my own dad that I had gotten sober. I'm afraid of being embarrassed. I don't want people to see the weak side of me. What if I fail? What if I don't finish? All things that sobriety would teach me how to handle along the way, but at this point in time, I was terrified.

At about the same time, I found out that my cousin was doing a race in Philadelphia called the Broad Street Run. It's a ten-mile run that runs from neighborhood to neighborhood, right through the center of Philly. My cousin had also gotten sober a few years before me. He was also bigger than me. I was about 225 pounds, and he I think he was about 265. (Sorry, Joe, if I'm way off!) I had seen him at a family party and talked to him about it. He told me that he had been running for a while and that I should buy a book by Jeff Galloway called *Galloway's*

Book on Running. What intrigued me about the book was how my cousin described it. He said Mr. Galloway had him run a mile and then walk a minute. Repeat, repeat, repeat. I loved that. It sounded like I didn't have to be a sprinter on day one. So I bought the book.

One of the first things he said in the book is that people try to do too much too fast. They are out of breath and their whole body hurts, and then they quit. That was a picture-perfect example of me. I knew exactly what he meant. That had happened to me at least twenty different times trying to run. So I read his book and listened to what he had to say. One of the lessons that I hope people learn from reading this book and something that I will continue to point out is that that the answers are all there for you if you listen. Sometimes they come quickly; sometimes they come slowly. The idea is that you listen, learn, and keep trying. (Put one foot in front of the other.) Something simple like a man in a class telling me if I trained for a marathon that I, too, could do it stuck with me. Something simple like someone saying, "Of course you're winded; you just started doing this," gave me hope. People say that everything happens for a reason. That's true; you never know when you are going to use what you learned. The important part is that you put it in the vault and use it when you need it.

So I did it. I signed up for the Philadelphia Half-Marathon, 13.1 miles. I don't remember the exact day, but I remember starting a fifteen-week training program that I had gotten from Galloway's book. Each workout killed me, but I kept at it. He had me running thirty minutes on Tuesdays and Thursdays with a long run each weekend. At first, I ran until I couldn't anymore then I walked. When I caught my breath and could feel my legs again, I started running. Each week, the running became more, and the walking became less until one day, I finally started running all the times I was supposed to and walking only one minute every mile.

At that time, I lived near Valley Forge National Park, which is a gorgeous national park with a five-mile paved path around it. They still have some of the old log cabins where Washington and his men stayed during the Revolutionary War. I would meet my sober friends every Sunday morning and then go to the park afterwards and run. I'll never forget the first time I put five miles on my legs, seven miles, ten miles. I would go to bed as if I had walked across Alaska. My wife would look at me and half laugh and half cry. I wouldn't be able to walk for two days afterwards. But I kept going. Each week, I added a mile. Each week, something different hurt. I signed up for this race and told people, so I had to keep going. It wasn't until a few years later that I realized it wasn't me. A friend of mine came home from Ohio over the holidays. I took him on a run in Valley Forge, and he told me it was the hardest run he had ever done. Turns out that Valley Forge is a really tough run with lots of hills. I thought it was me. This guy was in shape. He had done a 3:10 marathon in Ohio, and Valley Forge beat him up. Again, lesson learned. It wasn't just hard for me. It was hard period. It's amazing how many things my mind will make up that aren't true. Again, just put one foot in front of the other; don't get distracted by the noise, and if you do, ask for help.

As things were progressing for me, I realized that I had never done a race before. I know it sounds stupid, but I didn't know what race day would be like, and Philadelphia is not exactly a small city. I think they get around thirty thousand participants for the Philadelphia half and full marathons. I didn't want to be walking around the city trying to figure it all out at 6:00 a.m. on race morning. So I signed up for a local 5K, which is about three miles. At the time, running three miles was still not that easy for me. I was still big and slow and not breaking any records.

This 5K was in my backyard. The local library was sponsoring a "Mary Smith 5K" (I can't remember what the real name was). It was for a guy whose beloved mother had died. It was his way of remembering her. I would say there were about fifty people there. It started at the town park, weaved through the neighborhood, around the high school track, and back to the park. I literally walked there from my house that morning.

When I got there, I got my first lesson. Get your race packet, and don't bring anything you don't want to throw away. There aren't exactly lockers at these races. They handed me my number, a T-shirt, and a packet of info. I proceeded to pin my number on right there at the table. I read all of the stuff that they gave out and then put it in the trash and threw the T-shirt over my shoulder. This was my first race, and I was getting a T-shirt!

Once the race started, I just ran with everyone else. The field was made up of forty-nine regular moms and dads and teachers and policeman, doctors and lawyers, and one moron who came to win the money. This strapper showed up in his short shorts and gray New Balance shoes. He looked like a porn star from the '70s with wavy hair and a mustache. I heard the starting gun go off, and that was the last I saw of him.

The rest of us *normal* people all ran together. Most of us were not that fast. In fact, I was near the front. There was not a single part of me that had any intention of doing anything other than finishing. I didn't care when or how. I just wanted to finish. By and large, the race went great. After about the first 1.5 miles, we actually ran right by my house. It was funny because as we passed it, I had balled the T-shirt up that was still over my shoulder and threw it onto my driveway. It must have been obvious that I lived there, but it was funny nonetheless. Unfortunately, my driveway wouldn't be there for the big race.

I was hurting a little bit in the second half because I didn't realize at the time that my adrenaline had me going beyond my ability, especially once I got to the hills. Small as they were, they were still hills to me. Me and another guy my size traded passes with each other. I would whiz by him on the flats and downhill, and he would slowly pass me as I struggled up each hill. I'm sure it was a real Olympic moment to watch. In the end, I finished fifth, probably the highest I will ever finish in a race. I'm not being negative; it's just reality. I'm six foot three inches tall and two hundred plus pounds. I'm not going to be a race winner. I actually should have finished fourth, but there was a girl in front of me on a narrow path, and I thought it would have been demoralizing for her to have me fly by her at the very end. I know; I'm just like my mother. I feel bad for everyone. I know where I finished. That's all that mattered to me.

Sitting on the other side of that finish line was a monumental accomplishment for me. Not being able to run a full lap around the track less than a year before made it feel even that much better. We all sat there eating our bananas and drinking water. Half of the people knew each other, but despite the fact that it was in my neighborhood, I knew no one. I guess I lived on the "non-exercising" street.

Getting to the finish line was a baby step. It showed me a lot of things. I didn't know what the process was for a race, so I signed up and found out. I didn't know what it was like to run with other people, but I found out. I found out that I needed to start practicing more on some hills. I also found out that I could do it. I just had to try.

A few months had gone by, and it was half-marathon time. Was I ready? Would I be able to do it? Would I die of embarrassment? Unlike the 5K, for this race you had to pick up your packet the day before. I guess it's not that big of a deal when you have fifty people, but it would probably get a bit messy if thirty thousand people all showed up at 6:00 a.m. on race morning to pick up their packets. I took my four-year-old daughter with me. After standing in line for fifteen minutes or so, we walked through the gigantic tent and looked at all of the merchandise for sale. The first thing that struck me was the sheer amount of people there. There were thousands everywhere. And it wasn't even race day. I had spent the majority of my life making fun of half of these people while I drank away all my sorrows, only to find myself standing there envying them.

One of the things that I had decided early on was to expose the kids to exercise at an early age. While I don't make them do anything and they are very "girly," I want them to see what it's like to lead a healthy life. I have actually kidded with my wife that I am going to make both girls run a 5K when they turn eighteen to show them what hard work and putting your mind to something can accomplish. Only time with tell if they become interested. I don't care if they run races or do triathlons; I just want them to lead healthy lives and not just sit on the couch eating junk and playing Xbox.

Emily and I had had enough of the tent, especially her. Four-year-olds don't tend to have a very long attention span. So we left.

I spent the better part of the day panicking about the race, not even so much about the race itself as much as the whole thing. Would I finish? What if I didn't? What if I got cramps? You name it, I worried about it. I must have drunk about ten gallons of Gatorade that day. This was well before I spent anytime whatsoever on nutrition. I have always been an exerciser but almost never have I eaten properly in training. I don't eat Big Macs or anything like that; I just eat what I want to. I try to watch my weight, but those stinkin' Swiss rolls call me at night, especially when you are trying not to drink. I felt that if I drank enough Gatorade the day before, it would help me during the race.

The next morning, I got up at some ungodly hour and drove downtown. I got lucky and found a parking garage close to the race site so I could get out of town when the race was done. In typical John Toth fashion, I was way too early, even for a marathon that started at seven o'clock. I was probably there at five thirty. I managed to sit in the car for a while, but then my crazy mind kicked in and told me I better get to the race; otherwise, I might miss something.

One of the problems that alcoholics have is the fact that we isolate. I'm not sure why. Many of us can feel alone in a stadium full of people. You can be in a relationship with a wonderful person and still feel alone; it just goes with the territory (another test if you're not sure you're an alcoholic). Having this problem has been a pain in the butt, especially at races. I can be very social and the life of the party when the stars are lined up the way I like them to be, but if you put me in a situation that puts me out of my comfort zone, forget about it.

Want to see a neat magic trick? Put me in a place with thirty thousand other racers, and see how I manage to talk to none of them. That's right. None. I spent the whole pre-race walking around. I often find myself in the situation where I try to look like I know where I am going. I even mouth things to myself so that the person next to me thinks that I'm not just wandering aimlessly. I did that about thirty times. I would go from the tent to the bathroom to the starting line and back and forth over and over. Clearly, I have an issue. The important thing is that I did it. That discomfort that I feel a lot didn't keep me from doing the race. As the race got closer and we all took our spots, I may have even nodded to a few people.

Bang!

The starting pistol went off, and we just stood there. I guess it had never really crossed my mind that thirty thousand can't possibly all take their first stride at the same time. I was back at the nine or ten minute/mile pace so the "real" runners at the front were a good 150 yards in front of us. In fact, when we finally started moving and I actually got to the starting line, the clock said 7:05.

The exhilaration and joy of being there was awesome. I didn't realize how awesome it would feel, not only having trained and gotten there but also from being around so many healthy people. I have spent a fair amount of time with thirty thousand people, whether it was an Eagles game or a Phillies game. Never did I get the same vibe as I did from the race, and never had I been sober for it. There were all types of people, short, fat, tall, skinny, and every variation in between. We all had different backgrounds and reasons for being there, but in the end, we all had the same goal—to finish, to push ourselves to the finish line no matter what. There were thirty thousand different stories of how we got there and one goal. Some people had faster goals than others, but it was a camaraderie that I hadn't felt before, camaraderie that I felt from people I hadn't even talked to, if that makes any sense. I just felt good to be there. If only the FBI could see me now.

I made it through the first five miles without incident. It was so crowded that all I could pay attention to was passing people and getting passed. I wasn't even thinking about running or the fact that we were passing right through the center of town. I had a great view of the city from a place I wouldn't normally be able to stand. For all the criticism Philadelphia takes, it really is a great city.

After getting over the fact that of the thirty thousand people in the race, fifteen thousand of them seemed to need to pee in the first ten minutes, I settled in. I was amazed at how many spectators came to watch and cheer. I know that if I was drinking, I would have made fun of all those people cheering for people they didn't know. Having gone through it, I now know how much hearing some of those cheers meant.

We wound through the city and up through Drexel University. I remember seeing nothing but a sea of college kids all holding red Solo cups at seven thirty in the morning. I was very familiar with a red Solo cup.

We got through the colleges and up through Fairmount park. This was my first sign of weakness. My legs were starting to lose it, and we hit a big hill. Not wanting to chicken out, I killed myself to get up the hill. I think it was around mile eight. Around mile nine, I got a real kick in the butt. Because the Philly race runs both the half and full marathon at the same time, they have some sections for the full runners to run that will add distance to their race without making them run over to New Jersey. So they may have to run a half-mile loop that the half runners don't have to do. This really only happens during miles nine through thirteen. So for me, I came running down the hill after a really killer uphill climb, and the sign says mile 10.1. I was doing back flips. I was close, even if I had to crawl, I was going to finish. Then about five minutes later I looked up and saw a sign that said mile 9.2. I thought I was hallucinating until it happened again. All of the joy I had when I saw mile eleven was zapped out of me in a second when I saw a sign that said mile 10.1. What had happened was that because there was an additional loop for three or four miles, the half and full marathoners were running different distances. This was a killer for me.

My legs were starting to be done. I was starting to slow down a bit but was still running. One of the problems that I had that I didn't anticipate was that my body doesn't really like Gatorade that much. For some reason, it gives me acid indigestion. After about the second or third aid station, I switched to straight water, which, of course, is necessary but doesn't have any calories. One of the things that I didn't realize and probably my biggest mistake was that if you are going to run for two hours straight, your body needs fuel. As stupid as that sounds, I didn't know that. I thought just having water was all you needed. Not true! Obviously, I wasn't going to stop and get a hoagie, but it never occurred to me that I would have to keep adding calories to my body as I burned them. This had semi-disastrous results.

As I got to mile eleven, my body was kicking back. It was running on empty, and I didn't know it. I thought I was just tired from running. I started walking a lot more. I would walk for thirty seconds and then run for a few minutes. Repeat, repeat, repeat. I was getting cramps, and more and more people were passing me. That's very frustrating but something I would get used to. I made it through mile eleven and mile twelve. I remember as I came up to mile thirteen, I was really hurting. I was mad that the race actually had another tenth of a mile to go. Of course, that last tenth was up and around a hill in front of the Philadelphia art museum. This is where the finish line was and the bleachers for the fans.

The cheering alone got me up that hill without walking. I ran across the finish line but not before slowing down so that the couple in front of me could cross first. Not because I am a gentleman but because I wanted a picture by myself. I got one. I ran my first half-marathon in 2:06. Not bad for a big, slow, drunk guy that couldn't make it around the track without gasping for air.

The exhilaration I felt was indescribable. While I'm sure there were plenty of people at that race that day who had similar feelings, mine was different. It was personal to me. Had I had an ounce of energy left, I probably would have gotten emotional. As it was, I didn't. But I had accomplished something.

While there are many people that can run thirteen miles in their sleep, I can't. Every step that I took was a small victory. Thinking back to running on the beach with alcohol seeping out of my pores made it somewhat surreal. I had come a long way in the past twenty-four months and learned a lot about myself. With every challenge came a new lesson. Sobriety had taught me to block out all the noise in my head, all of those negative thoughts, all of those things that said, "I can't do this." I remember having a conversation with my friend, Frank. I was complaining about anything and everything. I wanted to be perfect in everything and be happy at every moment of my life. He said to me, "Sounds to me like you're looking for a finish line." Wow, was that a punch in the stomach. But it was true. I was. I was trying to line everything out in my head, in my life, in my job, to be perfect. I wanted to do the work and be done. What Frank so eloquently stated was that life was a long ballgame no matter what you are doing and that there was no finish line. You need to continue to work to be the best you can be and roll with the changes. Conversations like these are what enabled me to complete this race. It's because I was willing to listen to what other people had to say and apply it when I needed it.

ONE OF THE COOLEST
DADS I'VE EVER MET

After the Philly Half, I took it easy for a while. I wasn't one of those guys that picked up running and never stopped. I was glad to be done. The training wore me out, and winter was coming. All of the time I spent in the gym and on the track was quickly washed out by a steady diet of Thanksgiving, Christmas, and New Year's food. I wanted to take a rest but was putting the weight back on quickly. I have never really been fat, but I am a big guy. At my heaviest when I drank, I was 225 pounds, and not an ounce of it was muscle. That's just a lot of meat on a six-foot-three frame.

I spent the next few months casually exercising. I loved the fact that I could go out and run three miles without it killing me. Don't get me wrong; it hurt. I would be dying if I hadn't run in a while, but it was totally different. This time, I wasn't dying because my body was seeping a fifth of vodka through my pores. My ankles weren't hurting because they had atrophied from not doing anything for years.

After a few months of no real activity, I was starting not to feel so hot. I had again seen my cousin Joe at a family party, and he told me he was doing the Broad Street Run again this year. I had always wanted to do it, so I decided to sign up. The run was ten miles, and I had time to train. Since this race was actually three miles shorter than the half-marathon, I felt pretty good about it. It was also in May. There is something about exercising in the spring and the summer that makes you want to do it. I think the majority of us who aren't skiers hate winters.

I already had a training plan for this race. I was going to use the Galloway training plan that I had used for the half-marathon. Since I had already trained for a half-marathon and put the miles on my legs, this training went much smoother. One of the things that I have noticed over my years of exercising is that doing something for the first time hurts the most; that's why so many people quit. If you go to the gym and lift weights for a year, that first year is the hardest it will ever be. You are basically breaking your muscles and asking them to do something that they aren't used to. That's why you usually hurt so badly the first few weeks of a new exercise program. However, if you were to stop lifting weights for a year and then start again a year later, the second time that you started your training program wouldn't be as painful as the first. I've found that because you have already stretched those muscles and asked them to do those things before, your muscles tend to be much more agreeable the second time around. The body has a good memory with certain things, and this is one of them. So many people go to the gym and quit after the first couple of times. They try to do too much too fast, and it's painful, much like what Jeff Galloway talks about in his book. I always want to tell new people at the gym to stick with it past the first couple of weeks. Unfortunately, a lot of people think that it's only them and give up in February.

Because I had already nursed my legs back from near death for the half-marathon, I had no real hiccups during my training for the Broad Street Run. Everything went pretty smooth. I was still using the same running shoes I had bought for my training for the half, and I was still built like a linebacker.

As the race approached, I was getting a bit nervous. While I had now officially done two races, they had hardly undone the over thirty years of non-running that I had under my belt. I was starting to get nervous that the hills would be too big or that my cousin would be much faster than I was. While I was physically ready, I learned early that I had a long way to go mentally.

The Broad Street Run itself was awesome. I think the amazing thing about it is that it seems like most of the people there are actually from Philly. We start in North Philly and run through every sight and smell you can think of. From garbage to cheese steaks to Italian gravy, you get it all. For the most part, the run is relatively flat. Because of this, it draws all kinds of people, young, old, fat, thin, drunk, sober, people who have trained, and people who haven't trained in ten years. It's a big, fun event that gets bigger every year. I think the year that I did it, there were 22,000 people. That was actually my only complaint. There were too many people.

My cousin and I ran the race together. We stayed together the whole time. I am probably a bit faster than he is, mostly because he probably has thirty pounds on me. He's also just a big guy. But we stayed together. There were times when he was twenty yards ahead of me and vice versa, but we stopped at all the water stations together and kept close. Once we got close to the finish line, he had to walk for a little bit. The only reason I remember that is because I actually felt great, which was a first for me. I could have easily kept going. The adrenaline was pumping, and I loved it. But I waited for him. I waited for him because there was no reason in hell that I was crossing that finish line with anyone other than him. I had it planned in my head since the day I found out we were doing that race together. I knew exactly what I was going to do. I loved him like a brother, and here we were, two guys who a few years ago were the last ones at the bar, running down Broad Street at seven o'clock in the morning. We were usually the guys running down the street at 7:00 a.m. in Wildwood, New Jersey, coming back from an all-nighter.

So there we were, approaching the finish line; for every racer, there seemed to be five people cheering them on. It was great. As we got about twenty feet before the finish line, I grabbed my cousin's hand, held it in the air, and we both yelled. That's how we crossed the finish line.

The Broad Street Run was an amazing experience. Not only did I get to run the race and feel good, I could have kept running. I felt great. A lot of it was that my body was in better shape, and a lot of it was that I had my race day nutrition dialed in a bit better. I also got to run the race with my cousin. It really was a special moment that I am very grateful for.

I spent the next nine months doing my standard exercise. I didn't really have any kind of program. I would try yoga one day then run the next. There were periods of time where I did nothing but sit on the coach and eat Doritos. I may have gone a couple of months without running or lifting. I just did whatever I wanted. I was still going to a lot of twelve-step meetings. I was meeting other sober people who were golfers or played guitar. So I was always doing something. But I didn't have a specific regimen. One of the cool things about getting involved in recovery is that you get to meet other people who are like you, who share the same struggles and triumphs. That's one of the reasons they work. They make you realize you don't have to do it alone.

I was again starting to feel fat and out of shape. I knew that I needed to do something, but what? I don't know what it was, but the word triathlon had always sounded cool to me. I had worked with a woman who had done a triathlon. She was recently divorced with no kids. She was trying to reinvent herself. From the first time I heard the word triathlon, it sounded like you immediately became cool just for doing one. Like everyone else, I had seen the Ironman on Wide World of Sports and thought those people were nuts. Therefore, I should do one!

Regardless of my inaccurate feelings about the triathlon, I had thought about doing one a few different times, but I always had an excuse. I didn't have a road bike or a pool, I wasn't very good at running, or the cost was too high. Prior to me getting sober and for my first couple of years after, the thought had always been in the back of my mind. But I always came up with a reason why "I couldn't" do it.

Fast forward to the following January; my company had its annual sales meeting with me and four hundred of my closest friends. Our meeting is usually located somewhere in the Northeast part of the country because that is where the highest concentration of people in our company are located. This particular year, it was in Hershey, Pennsylvania.

Each year, the presidents and CEOs of all the different divisions get up and do their thing. There are a lot of charts and PowerPoints and way too much eating and drinking, drinking which I would have been a part of only a couple of years before. I was always the life of the party and the last one at the bar talking someone into something, usually paying dearly for it the next day. I can remember how scared I was to go to my first sales meeting sober. I panicked about it for weeks. I had spent the better part of the previous six months avoiding people, places, and things, and this was all of them rolled into one. I had a lot of sleepless nights worrying about that meeting. Lucky for me, it wasn't as bad as I had projected. I brought a lot of phone numbers of people that I could call if I got nervous or felt like drinking. I didn't need them. In the end I only called one person, my dad. All I told him was that I was fine and that the thought of it was worse than the meeting itself. Lesson learned. I took direction from other sober people, listened to what they said, and in the end I was fine. Left to my own devices, I'm sure I could have come up with a reason to drink.

It's kind of funny, actually, going to a work event sober. Instead of being one of those drunken, sloppy messes, I just people watch, which is its own reward. I love it when people show up for an 8:00 a.m. meeting the next morning looking like death. I always say the worst thing you can say to someone who is hung over after a night of drinking, "I feel great this morning."

One of the nice things that my company does each year for us at these meetings is bring in a few motivational speakers. Still the best motivational speaker I have ever seen was Eric Weinmeyer. He is a blind guy who climbed Mt. Everest. He was absolutely amazing. I remember standing up at the end applauding, and there wasn't a dry eye in the house, including mine.

This particular year, I had the honor of hearing and meeting Dick Hoyt from Team Hoyt. Most people have either heard of or seen Dick Hoyt on television. He is the father who does triathlons and marathons with his adult paraplegic son, Rick. HBO has done a special on him, and his face has been in just about every inspirational story you've ever seen. Together, they have done hundreds of races from the Boston Marathon to the Ironman in Hawaii. Against all odds, they did it together.

While all of that may sound good, it is not even half as impressive as if you have seen it. Dick literally has to drag, push, or pull Rick around in a cart or boat. So in addition to him training and finishing these prestigious races, he was doing it with the added physical and mental weight of his 180-pound paraplegic son, who could not help propel himself in any way.

Dick stood up in front of the auditorium and proceeded to tell us the story of how Rick was born and why he had cerebral palsy. He talked about growing up and all of the challenges that they both faced in everything they did. The thing that hit me the most besides the obviously amazing things he had done was that he was just an ordinary guy. He had a thick Boston accent, was about 5'9", and was built like a fireplug. He wasn't a particularly great speaker, but there wasn't a person in the room who missed a word he said. He talked about trying to enter the Boston Marathon and how the officials denied them access because they said he had an unfair advantage because Rick was in a cart with wheels. Here he was, a guy that had to run two bodies 26.2 miles, and they told him he had an unfair advantage.

He was not a professional speaker and was actually a little bit shy. But when he finished talking, there was a loud standing ovation and a tear in everyone's eye. I remember exactly where I was sitting and who I was next to. When they turned the lights on, I turned to my friend Sharon and said, "If he can do it, I have no excuse."

Dick spoke to us on a Saturday. By Monday morning, I was signed up for the Philadelphia Triathlon.

TRYING TO DROWN

Hearing Dick Hoyt speak was just the motivation I needed to get myself off the couch again. I have to admit that I knew nothing about triathlons at all. I mean seriously, nothing. I can't stress enough the fact that I am just a regular guy. I wasn't some star athlete just waiting to break out of his shell. I am athletic, but these people are a whole different breed.

The first thing I did was buy a book. It was either the dummies' or idiots' guide to triathlons. I read it cover to cover in a week. Like the half-marathon, I was told that I should sign up and tell a few people so that I would go though with it. So that's what I did. Now that I had signed up, I had to go through with it. I have amazing willpower sometimes and zero other times, which I guess is how I ended up with the title of this book. People think that alcoholics and addicts have no willpower, that's not true at all. We have unbelievable willpower in certain things; it's typically just in the wrong place.

If you're like me, you probably didn't know that there are multiple lengths of triathlons. Most people think that a triathlon is a triathlon. If you say you did an Ironman, people just think you swim, bike, and run but have no idea of the distances. There are many, and they vary greatly. The sprint distance has the most variation in distance and is usually around an 800-meter swim, a 12-25 mile bike ride, and a 3-mile run. The Olympic is double that. The Ironman is a total of 140.6 miles, and the half Ironman is 70.3. There are even a few others like Ironman lite and double-ironman. Amazingly, I had signed up for the right one, the sprint, a.k.a. the short one. I thought it would be a good idea for someone like me who couldn't make it a lap around the track to start with something small. You have to start somewhere. I was starting. I wasn't worried about anything other than that.

One of the fears that I had in doing a triathlon from the very beginning was cost. Unlike running, where you can just simply grab a pair of shoes and go, a triathlon had a lot of equipment. Although I had had these thoughts long before I signed up or bought the book, Dick Hoyt's story propelled me beyond that concern. But now here I was with some very real costs and very real concerns.

I knew there were certain things I needed to have and certain things I didn't. I needed a bike, helmet, running shoes, goggle, and a place to swim. Luckily, I had an LA Fitness about two miles from my house, but it cost a few hundred dollars to sign up. For the bike, I used a mountain bike. That's what I had, so that's what I used, more on that later. For the run, I just needed shoes.

While I had some of the things that I needed, I still needed to purchase some necessities—a wetsuit, tri-shorts, a Livestrong shirt (I thought they were cool-looking), water bottles, water bottle holders, and the like. Overall, I probably spent about $500-$700. Some of that was necessary, and some of it was because I am insane about stuff like equipment. I need to have a good pair of shoes to perform well. Not sure if that is an alcoholic thought pattern or just a crazy John Toth thing. Nevertheless, I got what I thought I needed. You can probably get away with half of what I got for your first tri.

A couple weeks after buying the book, I had a plan. I only needed twelve weeks of training, according to the book. So I spent some time trying to get my body used to swimming, biking, and running. I didn't want day one of my training to be day one of me doing any of those three things.

I'll preface this part by saying that there are three main things that I did as a kid, swimming, biking, and playing guitar. In the summer, if it was sunny, I was in the pool. I spent a ton of time at the shore and at the local pool and was a decent swimmer. I was never on the swim team and probably couldn't actually do any official stroke well, but I could keep myself afloat.

The other thing I did even more than swim was bike. I was a BMX'er before it became fashionable. I built my own Mongoose bike, one part at a time. My friends and I spent all of our time on our bikes. In seventh and eighth grade, I rode my bike to and from school. We were on our bikes so much that we built a track in the woods behind my friend Greg's house. People from all over the area used to come and ride it. We were the "cool kids" that built the track. Even when I grew up and moved in with Jaime, we would actually go mountain biking on the weekends. So I wasn't really all that worried about the bike, despite the fact that I hadn't actually been on one in ten years.

The only other thing I really did growing up was play the guitar. I played hockey in grade school and high school but didn't really love it. I wanted to be a rock star. Unfortunately, playing guitar doesn't help you with any part of a triathlon.

Having joined a gym, I decided that it was time to start swimming. So I was there for the first time, bathing suit on, goggles at the ready. I have spent a lot of moments of my life in my head thinking about the way something was going to turn out only to not have it turn out that way. That's what happened with my first swim.

I had gone to the pool a few times to check it out but hadn't gotten up the nerve to actually get in yet. On this day, I had decided that I was going to do it. It's like anything else when you are the new guy; you walk out cautiously, making sure you don't offend anyone or "mess up their routine." I had a mental picture of how my first swim was going to go. I was going to get in, turn my head to the side, and freestyle my way across the pool like Michael Phelps.

I think it was a Monday night. I went when I thought there wouldn't be anyone around. I got in the pool and quickly found out that this three-foot pool had a lifeguard. *Great, someone watching me,* I thought. I put my goggles on and decided I was going to do it anyway.

I got in the pool and stood next to the wall, giddy with anticipation. I took a deep breath, and with one giant push I propelled myself toward the other end. Left, right, left, right. I was swimming! I kept swimming as hard as I could. Left, right, left, right. Then it happened. I was out of breath and out of gas. *Uh oh, I'm going to drown in a 3.5-foot pool,* I thought. So I stopped and stood up. To my chagrin, I had made it about twenty feet. Yes, all of that flapping and breathing, and I had made it twenty feet. I was crushed. *I can't swim,* I thought. *What am I going to do? I signed up for a triathlon, and I can't swim.*

So I tried again. I put my head down and made as many strokes as I could. It moved me another ten feet. So I stopped caught my breath and did that two more times until I reached the other side. I was now in a complete panic. What was I going to do? I signed up for this triathlon and even told a couple people about it.

I stood against that pool wall for what seemed like an eternity. My maiden voyage did not go as I had planned. I was expecting to look like a sailboat streaming across the water, and instead I looked like a shark trying to escape from a fishing net. Ungraceful would be the understatement of the century.

But I had been here before. I am used to not being able to do something like this. Just a couple of years ago, I couldn't make it around the track and managed to train myself to run a half marathon. I wasn't going to give up after one twenty-five-yard lap. Sobriety had taught me that I can do things that I'm not comfortable with. I just have to take direction and be willing to try. So I put my head down and tried it again. This time, I made it a bit farther but still had to stop. I was getting a lot of water up my nose and in my mouth. Bilateral breathing was not exactly coming easily to me.

I spent the next twenty minutes or so doing what I would call trudging along. I would equate my swimming that day with running in sand. I was moving, but it wasn't fast, and it wasn't pretty.

I got out of the water a bit down on myself. I was expecting great things, and it turned out far from that. I was worried that I was going to make a fool out of myself, plus the fact that my triathlon was in the Schuylkill River, which didn't have a 3.5-foot bottom.

What happened next is probably the reason I am writing this book. Sobriety and triathlon are a lot like life. You have some ups and some downs, but either way, you have to keep going. At that point in my swim, it would have been very easy for me to quit. But I didn't. I wasn't going to let something like a bad first swim deter me. I could swim. I knew I could swim. It was just a matter of practicing. I had a lot of bad first runs, too.

So I did what would become a theme of my recovery and triathlon and life. I asked for help. Asking for help was one of the single best things that I learned to do early on. I'm really a very shy sensitive guy. While I can have the outward appearance of being a strong, confident man, I am really a little boy trapped in a man's body. I have a ton of fear and self-doubt. Sobriety helped me overcome these things.

To help solve my problem, I went online to every forum I could find and asked questions. I read everything that I could about swimming. I know this might sound stupid, but I got myself a nose clip to keep the water out of my nose for the first couple of months, and that was one of the best things I did early on. Not only did it keep the water out of my nose, but it also made me realize that there are solutions to problems if you look for them. Instead of sitting there complaining about them or blaming someone else, I simply looked for the answer and found one. Sounds simple, right?

I kept practicing every other day. And I got better. I could eventually make it the whole length of the pool without stopping, then two lengths, then three. With each session, I got better. With each session, I got stronger and developed more confidence. My introduction to running had really helped me. I knew that I was trying to do too much too fast and that if I followed the same advice I had for running that I would be fine. Being in recovery allowed me to ask for help.

A little while later, I saw a guy swimming next to me at the gym with some kind of flotation device between his legs so I asked him what it was. He explained that it was a pull buoy and that it was helpful when practicing. So I looked it up online and bought one for $9 the following weekend. Little things like that made a tremendous difference. Only a year or so ago, I did a race with thirty thousand people and talked to no one; now here I was at the pool, talking to strangers.

It was a Saturday afternoon. I remember it like it was yesterday. I was cruising in my own lane. I was about twenty yards away from the wall. I remember literally smiling underwater. My muscles were burning a bit, but I was going to make it. I swam a few more strokes, and then it happened. I touched the wall.

Eight hundred meters! The exact length of my triathlon swim! It had taken me almost a month and a half, but with hard work and not giving up, I was able to swim eight hundred meters without stopping. I pumped my fist to myself, just like I did when I ran my first mile. What a sense of accomplishment. To be able to put the time and work into something that you thought was not possible and be the only one who can truly appreciate the result is amazing. I think it's why most people do races. It's not the race that gives you the satisfaction but finishing the race as a result of all the hard work that you put in is what makes it so much sweeter.

One of my favorite sayings is, "If it were easy, everyone would do it." That's what makes those moments amazing. While there are probably thousands of people that could swim eight hundred meters with one hand while sipping a soda with the other, I am not one of those people. This was a challenge for me, and I did it. I asked questions, followed direction, and did the work. It felt almost as good as crossing the finish line in the half marathon, and I hadn't yet made it out of the pool of my local LA Fitness.

Sobriety continued to be a focal point in my life. I had seen enough people either drink or die after being sober for a while. I didn't want that to happen to me. I had a couple of years under my belt but was still struggling with the "living sober" part. My dad was right; putting the drink down *was* the easiest part. Now I was learning to live sober, and I'm not a fast learner.

I remember speaking to one of my sober friends one day when he jokingly said, "Life would be so much easier if everyone else behaved the way I want them to." While this may be an absurd statement to some people, to an alcoholic it actually makes sense. We struggle with things like this every day. We have a hard time letting things go. We let things get under our skin, and it eats us up inside. Then we drink. We don't like the way we feel, and our way of dealing with it is to medicate.

While I may have had all of the outward appearances of having it together, I was still emotionally struggling with my sobriety. I knew that taking a drink was not going to solve anything, but I was still having a tough time with how I felt inside.

Race day came sooner than I had hoped. Twelve weeks always sounds so far away, but like most things in life when you want the time to go slowly, it goes fast, and when you want it to go fast, it goes slowly. There must be something to that whole Yin/Yang thing.

The night before the race, I took my mountain bike out of the garage to put some WD-40 on the chain and the gears and wiped all of the ten-year-old mud off of her. I had literally ridden it twice during my training. All of my riding was done at the gym, probably not my best idea. Either way, I shined her up real nice and got all of the squeaks out. Then came my fatal mistake. For some reason, I thought it would be a good idea to adjust the gears on my bike the day before the race. It had been working okay but was getting stuck between gears once in a while. So I decided to adjust them. I will say that I am *fairly* mechanically inclined, but for some reason, bike gears are different. I can't seem to figure them out. Unfortunately for me, I never even got to the adjusting part; as soon as I clamped the wrench onto the gear cable, the end frayed. It was now virtually impossible for me to get a grip on it. What made matters worse was that in the process of trying to adjust it, it was now much worse than when I started. I went from having eighteen reasonably functioning gears to now having two. By the time it was all said and done, I had basically stripped the end of the cable, rendering it totally useless. So there I was, the day before my triathlon debut with a broken bike. All of that time and effort for nothing. What a waste!

As with everything in sobriety, you learn to step away from a situation and look at it realistically. I weighed all of my options and had finally settled on calling my old roommate Jamie. For some reason, since we lived together in the mid-nineties, we have always managed to live within a few miles of each other. In this case, he had just moved around the corner a few months before the race. So I placed a panicked call to Jaime and got his answering machine.

"Dude, I hope you're home, I don't care how late it is; please, please, please call me back."

That call was around lunchtime. I think when he finally called me back; it was around 7:00 p.m. He was calling from a rest stop in Washington, DC. He was on his way back from vacation. That meant that he wouldn't get home until at least 11:00 p.m. I didn't care; I needed a bike.

He called me when he got home, and I managed to pick the bike up just after 11:00 p.m. and breathed a huge sigh of relief, at least for the time being. Although I knew this before I called him, the one thing that didn't really hit me yet was that his bike was a full-suspension mountain bike, meaning it has shocks in the front and the back. Mine only had front shocks, and that was bad enough. Now I was doing a race on a pogo stick with wheels. Not to mention, it weighted about as much as a Dodge Neon. Nevertheless, I was grateful to still be doing the race, I think.

It was a beautiful morning in late June. The temperature was in the seventies, and there were plenty of people. I think about 1,800, if I remember correctly. In typical John Toth fashion, the race started at 8:00 a.m., and I was there at five thirty.

I parked what ended up being a country mile from where the actual race was. At least, that's what it felt like as I was lugging all of my stuff to transition. Transition is where you put all of your things during the race. Because there are three disciplines, you need a place to put your bike and run stuff while you are swimming and vice versa. For some ungodly reason, they have a rule that you can't actually ride your bike to transition, which is kind of ironic if you think about it, probably so you didn't kill anyone. Looking back, I can't even imagine what people must have thought when they saw me and my full-suspension mountain bike. I probably looked like something from *Sanford and Son*.

I arrived at the gates and got marked up. When you do triathlons, they write your number and age on your skin with a permanent black marker. I guess so if you get hit by a bus or die on the course, they can identify you. Because I was so early, I was able to get into the transition area and set my gear up with no problems. Now all I had to do was kill two hours worth of anxiety.

Despite the anxiety, I felt pretty confident about the race as a whole. I knew that I wouldn't be fast but thought that I could finish. Not including my new bike, the only real variable that I hadn't accounted for was my wetsuit. A few weeks before the race, I went over to the local bike store and bought myself a wetsuit. Notice I said bike store and not wetsuit store. Nevertheless, I browsed through the small triathlon section of the bike store and spoke to one of the young kids who worked there. I tried one on that seemed to fit me and ended up taking it home for a mere $300. One of the sayings they have about wetsuits is that "if it's comfortable, it's too big." I guess I fell for that theory.

I had planned on testing the wetsuit out in the water but for some reason had never done it. There is something about being the only idiot in the gym with a wetsuit on that made me a little skittish. The reason that I wanted to use the wetsuit was because it was supposed to give me extra buoyancy, thus making it a bit easier to swim. Combined with the fact that I was now going to be swimming in a river, I thought that it was a good idea. And it was, minus the not testing it out issue.

In hindsight, I don't think I did a whole heck of a lot right in my first triathlon, but nothing hurt me more than the swim. Not only was I now wearing a wetsuit that I hadn't practiced in, I hadn't even done a warm-up swim or ever swum in a river.

The cardinal rule in any kind of race is to never do it in a race unless you have done it during training. Don't try some new sports drink on the day of your race; it may upset your stomach. Don't wear new shoes on the day of your race; you may get blisters. Essentially, don't do anything that you haven't already done before and ruin your race, a lesson I apparently missed.

So there we were, standing on the fake beach next to the Schuylkill River, waiting for our turn. Unlike most running events, most triathlons start you off in waves, usually by age group. It makes sense. They want you to compete against people your own age, and it doesn't really make sense to have 1,800 people all start swimming at the same time. (More on this later.) Once the first wave goes off, you wait five to seven minutes for the second wave and so on.

I would have thought with all of those butterflies in my stomach that they would use their wings to help me swim. They didn't. My wave was finally called, and bang! We were off. I waited in the water at a level where I could stand so I didn't have to tread water. When the gun went off, I simply leaned forward and started swimming. *Wow, I'm floating,* I thought to myself. And I was. The wetsuit was really helping my stay afloat. So I put my head down and started swimming. I swam freestyle for the first fifty yards with no problem. Left, right, left, right. You get banged into and kicked a few times, but it's nothing major. The shortest distance between two points is a straight line, and everyone that is swimming is trying to get to that line. Everything was going just fine until I hit about seventy yards.

All of a sudden, I couldn't breathe. I could tell you the exact place I was in the water and exactly what I was near on the river bank. When I say I couldn't breathe, I mean I couldn't breathe. Imagine being in fourteen feet of water when all of a sudden you can't breathe and can't catch your breath. I started paddling immediately. I tried to doggy paddle and couldn't catch

THE ALCOHOLIC IRONMAN

my breath. I tried to roll onto my back. I still couldn't catch my breath. Panic. I was now in a very real situation where I couldn't breathe and couldn't touch the bottom. Every stoke I tried made it worse. I was just expending more energy without having any more breath. I tried backstroke, breast stroke, crawling. You name it, I tried it. I was starting to have a full-on panic attack.

I stuck my head out of the water long enough to see one of the kayak lifeguards about twenty-five yards away. I took off my swim cap (as is customary for people in trouble) and waved it at him. He darted his kayak over to me as fast as he could as I eked out a few more life-saving strokes. I reached up and grabbed the side of his kayak. I was petrified. I was out of breath and couldn't breathe. At that very moment, I thought I was out of the race. I remember holding onto the side of the kayak, telling him that I couldn't breathe.

I could hear another guard yelling to me, "You can do it, don't give up." But I was ready to. Staring up at the spectators on the side, I was so embarrassed. I was floating there seventy yards from the start almost crying. I kept thinking that I was going to have to call my wife, friends, dad, and coworkers and tell them I couldn't do it. It was a crushing feeling.

I couldn't figure out what had happened. I thought I could swim. I knew the wetsuit was a bit constricting and that the first half of the race was actually upstream, but this was bad. On top of all that, I started the race wearing the nosepiece. The problem with that was that when I really needed air, I couldn't get as much as I needed.

I held on to the side of the kayak for about three or four minutes. As long as he wasn't moving me forward, I was allowed to hold on. After some encouragement from him and my ego punching me in the stomach, I decided to keep going. My theory was that as long as I was within about twenty-five yards of a kayak, I should be all right.

For the rest of the swim, I was never able to freestyle for more than a few strokes without gasping for air. I would immediately lose my breath and start to panic. I did the majority of the race on my side crawling myself forward. It was by no means a fast way to move, but it was all I could do.

I stopped one more time on the final four hundred yards to catch my breath and clean my goggles. The volunteers at these races are really great. I always try to thank them as I go. I caught my breath long enough that I was able to make it home. It was an extremely long and physically draining swim for me. The final two hundred yards of the race were a diagonal swim upstream. That kicked my butt. But I kept going, crawling along.

When I finally made it to the swim finish, I was completely dejected, physically spent, and emotionally drained. Part of me wanted to cry, part of me wanted to scream, and part of me wanted to just go home. What I thought was going to take me twenty minutes ended up taking closer to forty-five and wasted about five times more energy than I had expected. I was completely out of gas.

I was so spent that it must have taken me five minutes just to get to my bike, which was less than a hundred yards away. I stopped at the aid station for some Gatorade. I remember getting out of the water and thinking, *Holy cow, I almost drowned.*

With what little energy I had left, I managed to pull myself together and get to my bike. I took my sweet time and pulled off my wetsuit, put on my gear, and *walked* out of transition. There wasn't a whole lot of traffic there, since just about everyone had already gotten their bikes and were on their way.

So there I was on my friend's full-suspension mountain bike with full, knobby tires, still shocked that I was alive. My original plan was to put street slicks on my bike, but I never got around to that either. Part of me was very relieved to be out of the water, and part of me was thinking that I was nuts as everyone was passing me on their $3,000 carbon fiber rocket ships. I thought I was actually holding my own for being on such a slow bike. That was until I got to the first hill. When I tell you I was on a pogo stick with wheels, I was. I stood up because of the size of the hill and pedaled my heart out. The problem was that for every foot I moved forward, I bounced another foot in the air because of the shocks. I was doing twice as much work as everyone else and going half as fast. I remember telling my wife and dad after the race that there were people that were a hundred pounds overweight passing me like I was parked.

In the end, I was still happy to be there. I didn't drown, and I was still sober. So I decided to just enjoy the bike ride for what it was, some exercise on a nice day.

I pulled into transition a fair amount of time after most people. By the time I got back there, most of the bikes were already re-racked, and people were already out running. I wasn't in last place, but I could tell there were only a few hundred people behind me.

For how poorly the swim and bike were, the run was fairly uneventful. I didn't do overly well in it, but given that I had wasted so much energy on the swim and the bike, I didn't really expect much. Again, I couldn't run a lap around the track a couple of years before, so everything at this point was a victory.

I stopped every half mile or so to get water and walk out the cramps in my legs. Surprisingly, given my lack of energy, I actually finished the race running. I wasn't going to walk across the finish line. It's kind of funny when you are that far back, half the finish line is gone, and half the bikes are already on cars and pulling out of the parking lot. I was usually fairly athletic, so most of the things that I did, even in gym class, had me finishing at least in the top half. Not here. In the world of endurance sports, size is not an asset.

Crossing the finish line filled me with a few different emotions. Part of me wanted to cry because I actually did it. Another part of me was still scared to death because I almost drowned. I was so scared by it that I didn't even know how to put it into words. I think I told my wife, "I had trouble with the swim." I was scared to death and thought I almost died.

My wife and kids greeted me as I crossed the finish line. My dad came down with them and cheered me on. I was part dazed and part exhausted. My six-year-old had gotten sick and was asleep on a blanket when I finished. I think my concern for her immediately washed away my fear for myself.

I learned so many lessons during my first triathlon that it's hard to list them all. I did things I never thought were possible. I challenged myself and overcame my fears. I even tried to drown myself. The fear of that moment was something that I wasn't sure I would ever outgrow. It's something I thought I would always think about. That was true, right up until the second, more successful attempt I had at drowning myself, my second triathlon.

Trying to
Drown Again

If at first you don't succeed, try and try again.

The summer had passed, and the distant memory of my first triathlon was withering away with the fall leaves. Once the triathlon was done, I hadn't really kept myself in great shape. I hadn't slacked off all together, but going from exercising six days a week to one or two was starting to show. Of course, I had to wait until Thanksgiving and Christmas were over before I decided to stop eating like a pig and get back on the wagon.

For me, I often base my exercise and diet decisions on the way I feel. When I start eating bad and putting on a few extra pounds, I feel like crap, so I want to start exercising again. It's like that feeling you get when you leave the Chinese buffet. It sounded like a good idea on the way in…

I hadn't really thought about anything triathlon related in a few months. To be honest, I'm not even sure what spurred it on again. But one day, I found myself deciding to do another one. Maybe it was to get back in shape; maybe it was to prove that I could do it. In either case, I was ready to do something.

Unlike the previous triathlon, I had decided to do an Olympic-distance race this time, the New Jersey State Olympic Triathlon. This race was twice the length with a one-mile swim, a 23.5-mile bike ride, and a six-mile run. Why I thought I could swim twice the distance that I almost drowned in the first time is beyond me.

I again used the triathlon book that I had bought to give me my training program. The training for this race started about a month earlier than the last one, which meant I was looking at about sixteen weeks of training instead of twelve. Although I had to put some more time into this race, I somewhat knew what to expect. I knew what my strengths and weaknesses were and what I really needed to work on.

One of the first things I did was buy a new bike. I sold a guitar that I had so my wife wouldn't shoot me for buying a $1,000 bike for a sport that I was only sort of involved in. I went online and found a Trek Equinox at a local bike store. It was the previous year's model, so I got it at a decent price.

Of course, I didn't get fitted or anything. I just sort of walked in and put the crossbar between my legs, and the sales guy and I agreed that it looked like it fit. Sold! After a short test ride, I knew this bike was way faster than what I currently had, so I walked out the door with it.

Riding that bike over the next several months was like riding a rocket with wheels. Believe it or not, it was almost a blessing to start off on the mountain bike, as it made me work harder and made this bike seem all that much faster. While you certainly don't need a road bike to do a race, it sure does help.

The next thing that I made sure to do this time was to practice in the wetsuit. While I still wasn't sure what had happened in the Philly Tri, there was a part of me that thought maybe it was the wetsuit, since I had been able to swim without one. Another part of me thought that it could have just been a panic attack from not being able to touch the bottom. I have found the further away you get from something, the less accurately you remember it.

The New Jersey State Triathlon was at the end of July. As part of my training, I had decided at the last minute that it would be a good idea for me to do the Philly Tri again as practice. It was a shorter distance but would give me more practice with open-water swimming and my transitions. The Philly Tri was about a month before at the end of June and fit perfectly into my training schedule.

About two weeks prior to the sprint race, I decided to try out my wetsuit in the pool. I'm not sure why, but I had the day off, so I packed up the suit and went to the gym. I actually went to a gym that was a bit farther from my house because I thought that if the people at my gym saw me in a wetsuit dressed like Batman, they would think I was nuts.

I got to the pool at a discreet time and hopped in the water with the wetsuit on. The first thing that I realized was how hot it was. Being in an 80-degree pool with a neoprene wetsuit on can get hot fast. It's an easy way to overheat yourself if you are not careful.

I started swimming and made it a few lengths of the pool, and it didn't seem to be too bad. I was swimming okay, even though I could tell that it somewhat restricted my arms. I probably spent a total of ten to fifteen minutes in the suit before it got too hot. I felt that that was long enough to tell whether or not I could swim in the wetsuit. I felt that I could. We would soon find out.

Fast forward to June and my second Philadelphia Sprint Triathlon. As I did the last time, I arrived too early and was the first one in my row in transition. I felt much better about this race than the previous one. I knew what to expect, and that's half the battle. Fear of the unknown is what gets a lot of us.

I got myself all set up in transition and couldn't wait to get out there. I thought my new bike was going to make all the difference.

One thing that I did this time that I hadn't done before was a practice swim. I thought that this may have been my problem the last time. I put my wetsuit on about an hour before the race and jumped into the water. Being that it was practice, I probably only spent about five minutes in the water at best. It was more to get comfortable in the wetsuit and see how I felt. I felt good, not great but good.

Waiting for the start of a race is agonizing. Not only do you have the butterflies dancing in your stomach, but if you are like me, you look at the start of that race as your start time. For example, the website says race starts at 8:00 a.m. So my brain thinks that the race starts for me at 8:00 a.m. But since the race starts in waves, that's not really the case. I think for this race, I was in wave sixteen. Assuming that the waves are about eight minutes apart, you can do the math and figure out that I didn't get into the water until after nine. That's a lot time to sit with butterflies in your stomach, wondering if you can swim.

One of the cool things that happens in triathlons more than any of the other races that I've done is that you can make friends if you want to. People are always asking questions about training and gear. Since there are so many newcomers to the sport, everyone has an open-door policy. If you don't want to talk to anyone, that's fine, too. Unlike the Philadelphia Marathon, where I didn't talk to anyone, I had met a guy at this race who lived near me, and he and I killed most of the time talking. I guess I must have grown some since the half marathon. I remember before we got into the water asking him how long he thought the swim would take him. He said about twenty minutes. That's about what I was hoping for but didn't offer up that information.

After a lot of idle chitchat, the time had come for us to get in the water. I had made the decision to start off slow. I didn't want the same thing that happened to me last year to happen again. I didn't want to jump out of the chute too fast and then spend the whole race swimming uphill.

After hours of excruciating anxiety, the time had finally come. Bang! Off went the starter's pistol. I started out at a nice, comfortable pace. I was doing freestyle and breathing fine. One of the things you don't realize when swimming in a crowd is the extra energy you use. When you are practice swimming, you can move at your own pace, stop if you need to and don't have to be embarrassed if you are already out of breath. When you are moving with the crowd, you can abandon your plan just to keep up and not bruise your ego. The same thing happens to me in a running race. I'm paying attention to everyone else and not to myself. I let me pride get in the way of common sense sometimes.

Things were going fine for about the first fifty yards. Then it happened, the same thing that happened the last time. I was out of breath and couldn't catch it. I was forced to grab a kayak sooner than I did the last time. I was so mad. I swore I had prepared. I swam harder in my practice sessions. Sure we were swimming upstream the day after it rained, but everyone else was doing it. I couldn't figure out what the problem was. Was it me? Was it the wetsuit? Was I panicking? All of the above?

After a quick kayak pit stop, I decided to keep going, knowing that I had completed the swim the previous year. I didn't have the same thoughts that I did the previous year that I couldn't do it and that I would be embarrassed. In hindsight, I kind of wished I had.

Not feeling overly worried after my first out-of-breath experience, I left the first kayak and started swimming again, trying to freestyle as much as I could. This time, I made it another fifty yards and had to stop again. I was completely out of breath. I couldn't believe it. I had already stopped twice in the first five minutes. I was getting really mad. I could also tell that my body was not into being in the water. I couldn't breathe again, but I was too stubborn to stop. In both cases, ambitious lifeguards told me that I could do it. So I kept trying.

I hopped off kayak number two and started swimming again. I was now looking at things in hundred-yard increments. I felt if I could do a hundred yards at a time, even if I had to stop at a kayak each time, that it would get me to the finish line. Again, not my best plan. The losing side of not being able to make it a hundred yards is that you drown, a thought I somehow missed.

I really struggled to get the next hundred yards. I actually ended up grabbing onto the bridge support in the water about seventy-five yards in. Again, I couldn't breathe and couldn't catch my breath. I felt like my whole chest was collapsing. Again, I waited to catch my breath, and I moved forward.

Each time I encountered a lifeguard, they would all say the same thing, "You can do it; the second half is downstream." I kept thinking if I could just get to the turnaround, I would be home free.

After another stop, I started downstream. It was definitely a bit easier, but I was starting to run out of gas. It was a real struggle to get to where I was. It probably took me about twenty to twenty-five minutes to complete half the course, while everyone else was finishing in that time. I was physically not ready to be in the water that long.

I made only one more stop on the downstream leg of the course; I cleaned my goggles and caught my breath. I swam from there to what would be my final kayak. I can honestly say that during every hundred yards, every stroke was a true struggle. As with my previous race, the last two hundred yards of the course had me swimming diagonally upstream. It's really more like swimming from one side of the river to the other on a slight diagonal. That means a couple of things. Not only was I swimming upstream, I was swimming twice as hard to not end up downstream and have to swim back up to make up the difference. And did I mention this was at the end of the swim? Brilliant.

I had stopped at the last kayak to catch my breath. I was only there for about thirty seconds when someone else in the water called for help. That meant that the kayak lady had to ditch me. It wasn't so much that she ditched me as we just kind of broke apart because I wasn't actually drowning and that guy was.

I remember having looked to the shore from where I was. It was a couple hundred yards. I told myself that I was just going to suck it up and make it the full way to the finish. I can't remember if I knew this ahead of time or realized it too late, but that kayak I grabbed was the last one on the course. I guess they don't normally position any rescue boats near the end, as they figure if you made it this far, you probably aren't going to drown. I would challenge that theory.

I made it about one-third of the way there before I started to lose my breath. I stopped and looked around and realized there were no kayaks anywhere near me. Holy smokes! So I put my head down and started to swim harder toward shore. Funny thing about losing your breath, exerting more physical effort doesn't help you get it back faster.

I looked up, and I was a little more than halfway there. That's when I started alligator rolling. Don't ask me what that means; it's just what I felt like. I was so out of breath that I started rolling onto my back to backstroke then to my side. With each move, I was exerting more energy, thus becoming shorter and shorter of breath. It is a very powerless feeling to be stuck in water with no air and no gas left, all the while being only a hundred feet from two thousand fans who can do nothing but watch.

At this point, I was starting to panic. Aside from being out of gas, I was now getting that, "Oh my God, I might drown," panic in my stomach. When I say that I thought I was going to drown, I mean it. I was starting to hyperventilate; I was flailing around. Had I been able to yell for help or thought that someone near me could have helped, I would have yelled. I was floundering in the water, looking up at the fans and thinking that there was nothing they could do. I got to the point where I finally had to do it. I had to yell for help. I was about thirty feet from the shore and just yelled help to one of the volunteers. I barely had enough wind to do that, and he could barely hear me. I could see the panic in his eyes when he finally realized how much trouble I was in. I pulled my head out of the water again to see him frantically taking off his shoes. He jumped into the water about chest deep in all his clothes. I reached for him, and he reached for me. We locked hands, and he pulled as hard as he could. He pulled me up until I could touch ground. That guy saved my life. I was scared to death.

I was so physically spent and mentally exhausted I said thank you and then immediately sat down. I didn't even have enough energy to walk up the fifteen-foot sand ramp to transition. I sat down, and they called for medical. The medical people came down and asked me if I needed anything. I said, "No, just unzip me. I can't breathe." I sat there for a good five minutes catching my breath and dying inside that I almost drowned. I remember thinking that I was going to have to call my wife and tell her that I couldn't do the New Jersey Olympic race because I couldn't swim. I was really upset, mostly because I could have died. I was in such a daze, I never had a chance to really thank the guy that saved my life. So, "Thank you, whoever you are!"

After about five minutes, I caught my breath. I decided that as I was here and on land, I might as well continue. So I did. I stood up and walked over to transition. As expected, most of the bikes around me were gone. I really took my time, took off the wetsuit, and got my bike gear on. The nice thing about being one of the last people out of the water is that you have transition all to yourself.

For all of the commotion and fear that came from the swim, I ended up having a great bike ride. Part of it was because I was now on an actual road bike, and part of it was because of my training for the longer distance. I was whizzing by people, and I felt great. Unlike the previous year, when people were passing me like I was going in reverse, when all was said and done, I beat my previous year's time by about eighteen minutes. I was totally thrilled to have something positive to build on.

Having an awful swim not only affected my swim and overall time, but it really affected my run. Although I had pushed reasonably hard on the bike, I could tell it was the swim that did me in. Like the previous race, I had planned on running each mile with a one-minute walk break between each mile. That was not meant to be on this day. I don't remember how far I got into the run, but my legs started cramping up fairly quickly. I was getting cramps in places that I didn't usually get cramps and could tell it was from struggling to keep myself afloat in the water. Not only was I using my arms, I was also kicking my legs much more than I am used to. Drowning will do that to you. Combined with the fact that I still had no real nutrition plan, I was a mess.

The run was fairly uneventful. Overall, I think I probably ran three to four minutes then stopped to walk off the cramps I was getting. It's a weird thing getting a cramp in your hamstring and your quad at the same time. When you pull your leg one way to stretch it out, the other side locks up and vice versa.

With about a quarter mile to go, another big guy looked over and said to me, "Come on; run in with me." So we did. We didn't speak much, but he was looking for someone to help him finish, and I needed the motivation. The last two or three minutes of that race were brutal, but I didn't stop. I didn't want a guy who was fifty pounds heavier than me to kick my butt.

Some of his buddies greeted him fifty yards before the finish line, so I dropped back and let them have their moment. I crossed the finish line partly relieved and partly disgusted. All of me was still freaked out by the water incident. I was still scared to death.

Over the previous two hours, I had made a decision that this was my last triathlon. I really enjoyed them, and I liked the training, but I didn't want to risk drowning; I had a family. I sent my wife a text and told her that I finished. Then a little while later, I sent her another one saying I was dropping out of the New Jersey State Triathlon.

Asking for Help!

I have said over and over again that asking for help is one of the greatest things you can ever learn to do. I really mean that. It took me being a drunk to get that. I remember when I first got into recovery telling someone something and thinking that I was the only person in the world who thought that way. Then he looked at me like I had two heads and said, "Yeah, we all think that." I know that might sound stupid, but it took recovery to point out to me that a lot of people think the same things; we just keep them buried inside.

One of the things that recovery forces us to do is to look at ourselves. We don't have the luxury of ignoring our character defects or our flaws. If we do, they end up festering inside of us, and we could end up drunk. We are forced to learn to face our problems instead of hiding from them. Too often I have seen people try to get sober on willpower alone, and it doesn't work.

At some point during all of my racing and trying to fix myself physically I realized that I was still an emotional wreck. I didn't just put the drink down one day and that was it. I struggled like everyone else does. Some days were better than others and some days much worse. In most cases I never really came close to a drink, but I was far from cured. One of the things that I wasn't prepared for when I got sober was how raw my nerves had become. I could fly off the handle at the smallest thing or be the most peaceful person you ever met. That's what they call living sober; learning how to live life. Life wasn't going to stand still and wait for me. I had to learn how to deal with it. At some point someone had explained to me that I never really learned how to deal with things because I always drank my feelings away. That was true. Whether the feelings were good bad or somewhere in between, I had a reason to drink because I didn't like the way that I felt. Now that I was sober I had to deal with those feelings without the help of a drink. Something that I will probably struggle with the rest of my life.

While I had spent most of my free time with guys like me who were trying to get sober, I was still an emotional train wreck. For some reason, my third year sober was the hardest. It was also my angriest. I don't know why, but I was angry at everything. Driving down the Pennsylvania Turnpike, I wanted to kill everyone. No one knew how to drive, and I somehow felt it was my job to tell them all. If you were in front of me in line at a supermarket with a phone attached to your ear, I wanted to grab the phone and put you through the front window. The list could go on and on.

At some point, I took some direction and decided that I needed more help than just my sober friends. While they were a great help, many of them struggled with similar issues. I needed real help. It was time to bring in the professionals.

A few of the guys that I knew had gone to a psychologist and raved about him. I think at the beginning I was either too macho or too scared to consider something like that. Much like how I got into recovery, I was beat up enough that I decided to give it a try.

My experience with therapy was a good one. I had a really cool guy name Frank B. It wasn't like I saw in the movies where they hooked me up to electrical wires or had me look at blobs of ink on a sheet of paper. My experience was simply me talking to Frank about how I felt. A lot of people get hung up on that. They don't want to show their feelings in front of another person, let alone a man. I didn't care. I knew that to some degree I was broken. My goal was to fix myself. Our society teaches us to never admit defeat, never show our weaknesses. Bigger, better, faster. That is not how sobriety works. Sobriety is about change. Half the battle is being willing and not letting your ego kill you.

For me, therapy was not about delving into the hidden meaning behind why I liked grapefruit juice. It was about talking about things with someone who was professionally trained. I'll never forget this one night. I sat down one night and complained and complained about someone. I listed fifty different reasons why they made me mad. When I got done, Frank just looked at me and said, "I would be mad about that too." I couldn't believe that he said that. As dumb as it sounds, I never knew that there were times when it was okay for me to be angry. What typically happened was that I got angry at something and then beat myself up emotionally about it for days. I would stop being angry about what had happened and just keep getting madder and madder at myself for not being able to control it. Frank's point was simply that you are in fact allowed to get mad at things. It's okay. It's holding on to things for days and weeks that's the problem. Having someone look at me and tell me it was okay really helped me.

I had told my wife vaguely what had happened in the water. I told her that I almost drowned but never really gave her the full picture. Part of me was embarrassed and another part scared. I did tell her that I needed drop out of the New Jersey state triathlon. I would rather lose a $135 entry fee than drown. That's exactly what I told her.

The rest of that night, I calmed down a bit. Still a bit freaked out, I knew not to make any irrational decisions. When I woke up the next day, I decided that I had put in too much time to just quit. If I tried to swim and got lessons and couldn't do it, that was one thing, but just quitting was not what I wanted to do. Life is full of moments like this. You hit bumps and have to decide what you are made of. I had decided that I didn't want to live the rest of my life regretting giving up. Something new to me. The next morning, I went into work and hopped on my favorite triathlon site, beginnertriathlete.com.

Here was my message:

> Well, this is my last resort. (Maybe it should have been my first.) I was intent on being a triathlete as I love the mix, but after my Sprint Tri this weekend in Philly, I'm questioning myself. This is my second sprint. I am in reasonable shape. I am actually training to do the New Jersey State Olympic in July so I thought I would be great for this. Well I wasn't. I'll start with last year. Last year I was a new swimmer. I trained in the pool but put the time in and thought I would do fine. I went out and paid $300 for a wetsuit and jumped in the river to do the swim. Within 90 seconds I had a panic attack. I couldn't catch my breath. It didn't matter if I flipped on my back, side, doggy paddle, etc. I thought I was going to drown. I finally flagged the kayak over and caught my breath. As the thoughts of all my family watching them pull me out of the water went through my head, I swore it was the wetsuit that was constricting my breathing. Anyway, I muscled my way through the swim. Took me a long time and I stopped at another kayak along the way. I may have been the last one in my age group (even though technically I should

have been a Clydesdale). When I got out of the water I swore I would never do that again. I really meant it.

Well, the winter and a few too many holiday parties and I forgot how bad the swim was. So I signed up for two. A sprint and an Oly. Well the Philly sprint was this weekend. I have been training for the Oly and spending a lot of time in the pool. I am more comfortable and can swim longer. I even practiced in the pool with the wetsuit once or twice. Well, the day came. I hopped in the water and did a warm up. My lungs were constricted but they warmed up. I did 50 yards or so and thought I would be fine. Then the start. As we entered the water, the woman at the bottom gets on the speaker and says "If you've never done this before, it's like swimming uphill." Great. We start; I try to pace myself. I get to about 100 yards and have to grab the kayak. I'm dying, can't catch my breath. I start again and get to the bridge and have to hold on to that, then another 100 yards and have to hold on to another kayak. It doesn't matter what I do, doggy paddle, lie on my back, side stroke, nothing works. I stop at the final kayak about 200 yards from the finish. I'm determined to put my head down and just freestyle my way in. I get about 100 yards and can't breathe, but of course there are no kayaks around now. I started to panic. I could see the shore and all the families. I could see the volunteers and was looking for a life preserver or something. I made my way to within about 20 yards of the shore when one of the volunteers saw me. I was seconds away from yelling "help." I could actually see him take his shoes off and jump into the water. He waded out about 10 yards and grabbed my hand. He helped me in. I sat on the sand and caught my breath for 3 minutes. I truly thought I was going to drown. I got on the bike and decided this was my last tri. I was not going to risk drowning again. Then I decided that I have trained too long and that I was not going to let this beat me. So here I am, asking for help. I have a feeling that it's the wetsuit. That it's too tight and I can't breathe. It may be the cold water. It may be the fact that I have the ability to put my feet down in the pool when I get tired. But I honestly feel that based on my training I should be able to regulate my breathing and do this. Does anyone have any ideas why I am having such a hard time? I've done half marathons etc and have decent lungs. This last one really scared me. I was always in the pool and the ocean as a kid and never had a feeling this close to drowning before. Please help if you can!

I got several replies from different people; suggestions ranging from spending more time in open water to getting a coach to it's all in my head. I was open to anything and wasn't discounting any theory.

I spent the better part of the next week researching swimming online. I read forums, articles, books, etc. One of the mottos that I had heard during my sobriety was, "The people that get it are the people that do the work," and I believed that. In sobriety and in life. I eventually found a website from a guy name Todd Wiley. Todd was a local triathlete and a coach. He was hosting an open water swim class at a lake about twenty-five minutes from my house. It was about two weeks before my Olympic tri in New Jersey. So I signed up, still not having dropped out of the race.

The weekend came for the swim class, and I packed all of my stuff into my car and made the trek to Todd's class. I was somewhat convinced that my problem was the wetsuit but wasn't 100 percent sure, so I brought it with me. After all, I had spent so much time in the pool I knew I could swim.

When I got to the lake, there were about fifty other people doing the class as well. It wasn't so much a class as it was a supervised swim. It's never a good idea to do open water swimming alone, due to the obvious drowning risks. This class gave you the ability to practice while having a few safety boats on the course, just what I needed.

I had sat in the car for about fifteen minutes before the class started debating whether or not I should wear the wetsuit. It was the middle of July, so it wasn't really necessary. However, I knew that the suit would help me float. After much discussion with myself, I decided that the last two times I wore it were a disaster; I was going to try this time without it.

Todd was a nice guy, and you could tell he was in shape. It pisses me off when you can see a guy's six-pack abs through his T-shirt. He also brought with him a woman named Jessica. They talked for about a half an hour and took questions from the crowd. It was helpful to hear that I was not miles apart in my head from what they were saying.

They broke the class up into two groups, those who just wanted to get out and have at it and those who "needed more instruction." That was code for saying, "We're going to stay near the shore where you can always touch bottom."

Still scared from the Philly Tri, I went with the beginner group. They started us out swimming about twenty-five yards along the shore in waist-deep water and then turning back around. I did it. No problem. Then we did it again. This time, it was fifty yards; again, no problem. We did each of them a few more times; each time, I got back to base first. I was feeling good.

The next part of the training was to swim out to a buoy and back. We were now leaving the safety of the shallow water. I did it with no problem. Up to that point, that was the farthest we had swum, probably about seventy-five yards. I still felt good. Then we did two buoys and made a triangle. I did that. Starting off slow was a great way for me to lose some of my fear. Had I just jumped into the water and tried to swim a half-mile, I probably would have freaked out again.

Then came the big moment. Jessica said, "Who wants to try to do the full half mile?" There was a full half-mile course set out in big orange cones around the lake. I raised my hand, as did most people. They decided to break us into thirds. There was another coach who was going to take me and a couple of other people out, as well as two others to take the other two groups out.

When I was given the go ahead, I was off. I have to be honest and say that I was slightly scared simply because being alone in the middle of a lake, where you can't touch the bottom, is scary. But I needed to do it. There was a safety boat there, and it was a lake, not a river.

I listened to what the coaches said and didn't go out too fast. They talked about going out really easy and taking overly exaggerated slow strokes to make sure you didn't get into a rhythm you couldn't sustain. I took very long strokes to make sure I was taking my time. One of the other important things that they suggested was to slow down when you got tired. It's no different than running. If you get tired, slow down until you catch your breath. Your body will still float and coast; just slow your strokes down. Again, I listened. Again, it worked.

I was about two hundred yards into the swim when I realized I could do it. I remember smiling underwater again. I stopped to see if I was supposed to wait for the coach and others to catch up to me. He was a hundred yards behind me waiting for the others and waved me on.

I put my head back in the water and went. I followed their advice. I swam my heart out; when I started to feel a little bit winded, I would slow down. When I felt better, I would speed up. I did the whole half-mile in fifteen or twenty minutes. It was great!

It was the wetsuit! It was the wetsuit! It was the wetsuit!

Without the wetsuit restricting my entire body, I was able to breathe and swim with relative ease. I knew I could do it! I'm so glad I didn't give up.

When I got to the finish area, everyone must have thought I was nuts. I was pumping my fist like I had just beaten Michael Phelps. To them, it was just some open water swimming; to me, I had faced a demon and overcame it. It was a big deal for me.

When I went to get out of the water, Todd was standing there talking to someone and said, "How do you feel?"

"Like a million dollars," I said.

"Good," he replied.

I felt like I had just scaled Mt. Everest. I was high as a kite. I did it. I was willing to take the necessary steps to make it happen. I was willing to embarrass myself on a forum and tell people I almost drowned. I was willing to ask for help. If it were up to just me, I would be sitting on my couch telling my wife and friends how stupid the sport of triathlon was and that I was going to focus on golf. But I didn't. I put one foot in front of the other and asked for help. It's amazing what happens when you do that.

ANOTHER RACE,
ANOTHER LESSON

THE NEW JERSEY STATE OLYMPIC TRIATHLON
Having done the open water swim class had really boosted my confidence. However, that was not in a race with other people, and this distance was twice as long. For the New Jersey State Tri, I needed to be able to swim a full mile with no wetsuit and keep myself afloat.

In typical John Toth fashion, I again showed up entirely too early. This time, I even brought my iPod and a book with me so that I would have something to do while I was waiting, but as usual, I just paced around. Most people would just show up later. Not me; I brought supplies.

I got to transition before the rooster crowed and got marked up. It was a weird feeling being there for the Olympic race. For some reason, I felt like this wasn't really playtime anymore. While there is really absolutely no truth to this, my mind somehow equated the sprint race with "beginner," while the Olympic was for "more advanced" people. Now I was in the middle of the "serious" people. There were $3,000 bikes everywhere I looked. There seemed to be a lot of people on teams and from tri-clubs and a lot of others who knew each other. I was there alone. I didn't want to make the whole family get up at 4:00 a.m. to see me run past them two times for five seconds apiece.

Waiting for a triathlon to start is like waiting to take your SATs. You've done all the preparation for it; now you just want to get it over with.

After racking my bike and checking and rechecking everything ten times, I made my way down to the swim start. Of course, for this particular race, the swim start was about a half a mile from transition. While you finished the swim near transition, you still had a bit of a walk to get to your bike.

I made my way down to the swim start for a practice swim. It was the first time I actually saw how far I had to swim. You could see the entire mile in orange buoys from the practice area. *Yikes, that looks long,* was all I could think. Luckily for me, I didn't get too wrapped up in it. I knew I had done the training and had a new confidence in the swim. "Just put one foot in front of the other," I kept telling myself.

So I hopped in the water and did a quick five-minute practice swim. I felt good; my lungs felt good, no big deal.

After watching some other people swim, I made my way back up to transition. One of the weird things they do at triathlons that I don't yet understand is close transition. For some reason, they want everyone out of the transition area an hour or so before the race starts. That means you have to take your swimsuit and goggles and that's it and hit the road. That means that about two thousand people all go down to the swim start at the same time and stand around in their bathing suits and tri-shorts.

I made my way down to the swim start and found myself a nice, grassy patch to sit down. I took a gel pack with me but realized when I got there that there were no water coolers. Eating a gel and not being able to wash it down with something isn't all that great. My fault; I should have been more prepared than that. Lesson learned. For those of you who haven't ever tried a gel, imagine eating a half a tube of Aim toothpaste but with a fruity flavor.

After what seemed like an eternity, the race director started his announcements. He did the obligatory speech about everyone having fun. He did, however, say something that will stick with me for a long time.

During his announcement, he said, "If you can swim, you can swim." He was trying to put people at ease. What he meant was if you can swim; don't panic because you can swim. If you're feeling anxious, realize it's just your head because you can swim. For some reason, that really stuck with me. I knew I could swim. That seemed to calm me down a bit. Little words of wisdom have such great power sometimes, if you let them.

After a few other words of encouragement, the race began. The sprint race started first. That meant we had to sit there for about an hour while we waited for wave after wave of people in the sprint race to start. Talk about torture. You end up being stiff, irritated, and generally annoyed. All I wanted to do was get out there.

After a few hundred Hail Marys and a new set of grass wrinkles on my back and butt, it was time to get in line. I stood up and downed my gel, still annoyed that I hadn't brought any water with me. After many nervous and tense moments, my wave was called to the water. Unlike the Philly tri, where the start line was literally ten yards into the water, the New Jersey Tri's start line was a good fifty to seventy yards in. You had two choices, you could either swim to the start and tread water or you could stand near the edge until the gun went off then start swimming a good fifty yards behind everyone else. I chose the latter. I decided that it was best not to throw myself into the blender just yet. Even though I had more confidence than before, I didn't want to push it. Plus, I was not trying to win; I was trying to finish without dying.

The gun went off. About a hundred people in my age group all started churning the water. I joined in. As the swim class had stressed, I started off slow. They said to over-emphasize your stroke, forcing yourself to slow down. That's just what I did. I kept saying to myself, "Slow, slow, take your time." I was feeling good swimming freestyle. The water wasn't too cold, and I found a nice outside lane where I wasn't smacking into anyone.

I made it about a hundred yards, and then it happened. My stomach. *Oh no! Not again,* I thought. I felt a huge swell of butterflies in my stomach. It felt similar to what had happened the last two times. I was about to start freaking out when I decided to calm down. I remembered what the coaches said, "If you're tired, slow down." So I did. I over-exaggerated my stroke and slowed down. Almost instantly, I was back to normal. "Listen, listen, listen" should be my new motto! The thought of not finishing the race had only been with me for a few seconds before I was able to pull out of it and keep swimming.

Once I got warmed up, I started to swim, at least, what I call starting to swim. I swam freestyle the whole race. A lot of people will get tired and doggy paddle. I did freestyle the whole time. I felt good the entire time and never had to stop because I was tired. I chose to swim on the outside of all of the people because there was less traffic there. Because of this, I probably ended up swimming a few hundred yards more than the other people, especially around the turns, but I didn't care. I would have rather done that than be smashing into everyone.

After my brief mishap with my overanxious stomach at the beginning, everything else went great. I found another guy (accidently) who seemed to have the same plan as me. He sort of hung around the outside and every once in a while, we would bump into each other, but it was more of an, "Oops, my fault this time," type of situation. All in all, I ended up stopping only twice to clean my goggles. After a while, they got so foggy that I didn't have a choice. I also got tapped on the head by one of the guards for going too far outside the swim lane. This was simply because I couldn't see. So I held onto her kayak and cleaned my goggles and kept going.

The last couple hundred yards were probably the hardest. As could be expected, I was getting tired. I wasn't in any danger like I was in Philly, but I could tell I was getting tired. I do remember thinking that if I had a boat next to me, I could probably do another lap, but that didn't exactly fit into my plan of finishing the race.

With all my might, I swam around the last turn and toward the finish line. Like they said in swim class, "Swim until your hand can touch the bottom." That's exactly what I did. I was slowly running out of gas but not even close to how I was in Philly, and this was twice the distance. I kept going until my hands could touch the bottom.

I have bad ears; they've been like that since I was a kid. When I get out of the pool sometimes, my equilibrium is a bit askew. So when I got out of the water, I took my time. I walked very slowly and even stopped for a minute. All of the hardcore triathletes were running out of the water like they had a chance to win. Not me. I stopped and stood there for about fifteen seconds, trying to make sure I had my bearings. After I was sure I wasn't going to fall, I crossed the finish mat, and my timing chip beeped. My official time was recorded as 39:53. In reality, I think that had I not stopped at the end or to clean my goggles, I would have done the whole thing in less than thirty-eight minutes. Considering that it took me at least that long to swim half that distance in both of the Philly tri's, I was ecstatic. It's all downhill from here.

Once I had gotten my bearings and crossed the timing mat, I made my way to transition. Unlike the Philly transition area, only about one quarter of it was on grass. The remaining quarter was on asphalt, old asphalt! I walked for a minute then decided I felt good enough to run, surprising even myself. I ran across that old asphalt, being extra careful to not slice my feet open. I made it to my bike a few moments later and proceeded to high five myself for being alive.

The rest of the race went fairly smoothly, minus a few mistakes. I like to call these mistakes teachable moments. In situations like this, I need to realize that I don't know everything and that I have to remain willing to be teachable, like when I tried to put my tight tri shirt on over my soaking wet skin. The people watching must have had a field day watching me hop around like I was trying to get out of a straight jacket. You have to learn to laugh at yourself.

My biggest mistake of the day turned out to be my diet. I guess I didn't realize it when I got into triathlons, but it is not a three-discipline sport; it's four, swimming, cycling, running, and nutrition. If you just want to swim in the pool and ride your bike a bit, it's no big deal. But the longer you go and the faster you want to be, you have to start paying attention to how to give your body the fuel it needs to continue. I had done the Philly half marathon on a can of Red Bull. I drank the can thirty minutes before the race, and that was it. No gels, no power bars, nothing. I didn't even drink Gatorade; I drank water the whole time. It wasn't until a few years later while doing triathlons that I realized why I was completely out of gas during the last two miles of that race.

Nutrition is a big deal, probably more so than swimming, biking, or running. I had started experimenting with gels and electrolyte drinks during the Broad Street Run and the sprints but hadn't quite perfected any of it. For the New Jersey Tri, I thought I was all that and a bag of chips. I had gels, Cliff shot blocks, and multiple water bottles. I had it all. I was a mobile buffet. Note the word *experimenting* above.

As soon as I got on the bike, I took a gel and things were fine. For some reason, I had read a lot about nutrition but not enough. I spent the next hour jamming as much water into my body as I could. It was a very hot day, and I thought that I had to do this not to dehydrate. I was guzzling water like I had been stranded on a desert island for a year. I felt great on the bike, and things were going fine.

One of my first mistakes on the bike was that I literally forget how long the bike part was. As unbelievable as it sounds, I wasn't actually sure how close I was to the finish because I forgot exactly how many miles it was. I was so worried about the swim, it never crossed my mind to look at the bike portion. The last time I probably saw the distance was the day I signed up for the race.

In addition to the water, my plan was to have some shot blocks to get some food in my stomach to fuel myself before the run. So I did. I had some gels, some shot blocks, some sports drink. I washed everything down with a ton of water, only to find that I was almost at the end of the bike. Minutes later, I was dumping my bike off at transition and starting to run.

For those of you who have never done this before, imagine eating Thanksgiving dinner and then going outside and running around the block as fast as you can. That's what it felt like.

I felt great for the first five or six minutes of the run. Then my stomach kicked in. Turns out the human body doesn't really like having a belly full of water and jellied sugar in it when it's trying to run six miles on a ninety-five-degree day. The one magical thing about the human body is that when it wants you to know something, it lets you know.

I made it to the first aid station without stopping, but that was when I realized that it was going to be a long six miles. My stomach was not going to put up with this. The smartest thing that I did all day was grab one of the wet towels that they had sitting in ice and wrap one around the back of my neck. At every aid station, I took two cups of water, one that I drank, and the other I poured on the towel. I felt like death, but at least I was staying somewhat cool.

The majority of the run was full of people complaining about the heat. I actually felt fine; the towel really worked. My problem was my stomach. My stomach was not happy. I was doing my best to hold everything in; it was doing its best to get it out. There were times where I thought I needed a porta-potty and others where I thought I was going to throw up. Either way, my stomach was winning.

To me, a triathlon is just another example of life and how things rarely go perfectly. The ones who do well are the ones who adapt the best. So after trying over and over to keep myself running, it was time to change strategy. I decided to run as far as I could and then walk until my stomach calmed down. When I felt okay walking, I would start running again.

It was kind of funny because there was another guy about my age doing his first tri. We kept trading places. When I walked, he ran, and vice versa. He was physically tired; I was just having stomach issues. Either way, we ended up joking about it. I would pass him, and he would say, "Tag, you're it," and vice versa. It was kind of nice, as it made me feel like it wasn't just me. As I said, one of the coolest things about these races is that you don't have to do them alone. If you want to, you can talk to someone virtually the whole race. Usually, people of the same skill level and background stick together. Although I'm not sure how many drunks there were in my section of the race.

After what seemed like the longest run of my life, I finally got back to where civilization was. For people that aren't familiar with Triathlon, the majority of the races aren't actually near people. Family, friends, and relatives all tend to huddle near the start/finish line. So when you are out on the bike or running, you don't really see many people, especially during the shorter-distance races. When you make it back near the finish line, it starts to feel like a race. You can hear the announcer, you hear the fans, and you start to feel the electricity. It's amazing how many people are there to cheer you on. With all the cheers and the cowbells, you can't help but get pumped up for the final quarter mile, which is exactly what I did. I passed my tag team partner and was on my way. I was dying but was not going to stop until I crossed the finish line. Thank God for all those strangers cheering me on. That's the only thing that got me through.

About two minutes later, I trudged my way across the finish line and heard the announcer say, "John Toth from Maple Glen, Pennsylvania."

I finished!

The exhilaration of finishing an endurance race is awesome. I always laugh when people talk about the runner's high. My comment to that is always, "Well if you hit yourself in the head with a hammer over and over for an hour, when you stop, you would probably feel awesome about not getting hit with a hammer anymore." I guess that is the skeptic in me.

Either way, I felt awesome. I think most of it comes from the fact that I put my mind to something, did the training, and accomplished the goal.

After a few bottles of water, a Coke, and a pretzel, I made the slow walk back to transition. I actually felt fine physically and a hundred times better than either of the Philly tri's. Had I not had the stomach issues, I think I would have done well. Another race, another lesson learned.

When I got back to transition, I had one simple goal, to text my wife and tell her that I was still alive. To be honest, I don't really deserve the wife I have. I am often very selfish, self-centered, and self-absorbed despite me telling the world what a nice guy I am. My wife is really the rock that holds the family together, even though she would never admit it. She is the reason that I am still alive and the reason I have the support that I need. Most of the time, when I blame her for something, it's really about me. I don't thank her enough for all that she does.

My text was simple. "I did it. I'm still alive!"

Having never really told her about the perils of my Philly tri swim sessions, she probably thought I was just being funny. I wasn't. I was happy to be alive and grateful for everything!

Leaving the race, I had a much better feeling than the previous two races I did. Maybe it had something to do with the fact that I didn't almost drown. I felt like a million dollars. I remember making the drive home to Pennsylvania and thinking how awesome I felt. I guess it showed me how it could feel if I didn't give up and kept putting one foot in front of the other.

Having completed the race, I felt that I needed to post an answer on beginnertriathlete.com about my swimming perils. After all, there were bound to be people like me that were having the same problem.

Here was my post:

> Yesterday I did my first Olympic. I'll write another post about that. Of course with the Oly you have to swim a full mile. I did an open-water swim class a few weeks ago, and it went great. Did it with no wetsuit and felt like a million $$$.
>
> Yesterday I did the same thing. That was my plan. I did two warm-up swims and felt fine. But as I stood there getting closer, I have to admit I was getting a little nervous. I had convinced myself that I was not going to panic. I *can swim*! Like the announcer said, "If you can swim, you can swim." I can swim. I wasn't overly nervous but I guess just anxious.

I did the smart thing and stayed to the back and right. Gun went off and I started. The one thing that the OWS coach stressed over and over, "Start slow." So I started slow. I didn't want to freak like the last two times. I felt fine. Everything went fine for the first 100 yards or so. Then I had a tiny nervous section. For some reason I got this weird feeling, it happened the other two times too. I think it's just realizing that your feet can't touch and you are way out there. I have this sudden thought of "oh no, I really can't do this." So I doggy paddled for about 10 seconds. Then it was back to freestyle. Not that this is a major newsflash, but for me freestyle takes way less energy than doggy paddle or treading water. So I started to Freestyle again and said to myself, "You're not really out of breath. If you are, slow down. You're doing fine." And that's just what I did. I got into a rhythm and everything went fine. I felt good. I realized after my tiny nervous session that I can do this, 'cause I can swim. Everything after that went fine. I swam the entire thing freestyle, only stopping once 'cause my goggles were so foggy I needed to stop to see where I was going. And another time because some girl decided to park her Kayak in front of me. I did the whole 1 mile swim freestyle in 39 minutes. I got out of the water like I had won the race.

The moral of the story other the all of the obvious (Don't give up, you can do it etc…), is that something as stupid as a mis-sized wetsuit almost made me give up. I love what the announcer said, "If you can swim, you can swim." Everyone told me to get some OWS practice in, so I did. If you're having trouble with something, here is the place to air it out. Someone here has gone through it. Hope this helps someone.

Now I'm onto another post to find out why my quads keep locking up during the run.

Signing Up, Ironman

I have heard people talk about it in articles and books before, but for me, the letdown after a race was simply that. I don't think it was depression or anxiety as much as you just don't know what to do with yourself and all the free time you now have. You spent all of that time in the pool and in the gym, and now you are free to eat as many ring dings as you want.

It didn't hit me right away; I want to say that it was a couple of weeks after my race. I was sitting on my back porch enjoying the summer air. I had been watching some of the Ironman highlights on NBC Universal at that time. I had this nagging thought in my head that I couldn't get rid of. At first, it started with doing a half-Ironman. I had contemplated actually trying to squeeze one in only four weeks after my Olympic since I was already in "decent shape." Lucky for me, I have always been logical. I realized that I would either be dying because I wasn't ready for the half or I would regret it because I wouldn't perform well. So I decided to hold off. I spent the next week or so with Ironman fever. I don't know where it came from or why; I just had it.

In case I have not made it abundantly clear yet in this book, I am not a world-class athlete. I didn't run, swim, or bike in high school or at any other point in my life. A few years ago, I was a drunk who couldn't make it around the high school track. Every foot I have made it in any race has been a struggle and a victory for me. Now I, a drunk from Philadelphia, had Ironman fever. Talk about crazy! If you would have asked me even three years ago if I could do an Ironman, I would have bet you everything I owned that it would never happen.

Now here I was, spending all my time at work surfing triathlon websites. I was watching Ironman programs on TV at home. I had gotten a taste of that feeling in my Olympic race and wanted more of it. I really don't know what came over me, but I was obsessed. I must have sat on my back porch for hours thinking about what to do. Then it hit me, why can't I do a full Ironman instead of a half?

Besides the fact that I am 6'3" and was now 215 pounds, I had some other things working against me, one being that I was thirty-nine years old. While in the grand scheme of things that's nothing, it doesn't exactly help you in an endurance sport full of people who eat tree bark and tofu. Another thing that I had working against me was the fact that I had a family. I'm not a young, single guy who could just take off a year from all his commitments and run away. I had to figure out how to do this and still stay involved with the family.

I knew I had been acting weird for a few days. I had a new purpose in my life. I felt alive. I felt like a kid waiting for Christmas next week. Here I was sober almost five years, not missing the alcohol but moving on with my life. I had spent so much time thinking about it that it finally just came out one day. "Honey, I want to do an Ironman." My wife knew there was something up for a while. She had watched me pace around and sit on the back porch for hours with my laptop going on forums and websites. I told her that I wanted to do it for my fortieth birthday; in truth, I think I just wanted to prove to myself that I could. Telling her lifted a huge weight off of my shoulders. I had Ironman fever bad. I imagine it was somewhat like women feel when they have baby fever. It's all you think about all day. For this drunken mess of a human being, this was quite a transformation.

Sometime in the next few days, I did it. I actually signed up for the Ironman in Lake Placid, New York. Living in Philadelphia, this was the only "official" Ironman race that I could drive to. Most of the other races in the USA are down South or out West. I didn't feel I needed the added stress and cost of trying to ship a bike somewhere. I knew it was already going to be a challenge; I didn't need anything else to add to it.

Again, wow! I just signed up for an Ironman. Even more amazing is that I paid money for this type of torture, $1,100 to be exact. I had to get into the race under what they called community slots, which means you pay double and they get to keep the other half for "the development of the sport." What that means in English is that the race was already sold out by other insane people like me who wanted to torture themselves and I had to use the secret handshake to get in. If you have ever watched the Ironman from Hawaii on TV, you can understand why (to some degree).

Now that I was in, I knew there were going to be a lot of things that I needed to take care of to make this happen. I was an alcoholic. Big and slow, not wealthy, full time job, kids, etc. After sitting on my back porch daydreaming about the Ironman, I was really doing it. I signed up. Now it was real. When I did my first half-marathon in my second year of sobriety, I worked with a woman who told me to sign up for the race and tell as many people as I could about it so that it would force me to follow through. I did sign up, but I didn't tell too many people about the Ironman. I didn't want to be embarrassed if I didn't finish. There was a much greater chance of that happening in this type of race. Anything can happen.

I wouldn't be completely truthful if I left out the part of me now being scared out of my mind. Somewhere within the first five minutes after I hit the submit button on the registration website, it hit me. "I just signed up for nine months of torture, something I am completely unqualified to do, something I have no experience at. Who do I think I am?" It became a metaphor for my sobriety. I don't have to know all the answers right now; just put one foot in front of the other.

Sitting on my back porch is where I first had the idea to write this book. When I tell you I couldn't run a lap around the track, I am not kidding. I thought that I needed to tell other people with addiction problems that there are other choices in life and other ways to occupy their time. I also wanted to show them that if you simply listen, ask questions, take guidance from people, and not pretend to know everything, you can succeed. I also realized that a lot of these things applied to life in general, not just sobriety.

Somewhere around the time I had decided to write this book, I had a brilliant thought (which, of course, depends on your definition of brilliant), *Maybe I could get sponsors to help me.* I knew I needed every ounce of help I could get to finish this race. Doing it on the road bike I had was not going to hurt me, but it wasn't going to make it any easier. The same held true for just about every other thing that I had. I had a lot of stuff but wasn't sure if it would help me get to my goal.

So I did it. I decided to see if I could get some sponsors. I sat down one day and came up with a sponsorship letter. I told people what I was trying to do and why and asked them if they wanted to help me.

Here is the exact letter I sent to the companies I hoped would sponsor me:

Dear Mr Smith,

My name is John Toth. I am a 39 year old Alcoholic. I have been sober going on 5 years. Recently I have gotten involved and fallen in love with the sport of triathlon. I have done several sprint and Olympic races over the past two seasons. I loved every minute of them.

Like anyone in the sport you have your ups and downs and lessons learned. I did my first sprint on a mountain bike. People were passing me like I was standing still. Lesson learned. I soon after bought a $1,000 Trek Equinox, mostly because I got a 2007 model in 2008 at a good discount. Boy did that make all of the difference on the bike. A road bike is certainly easier than a mountain bike.

Since the day I got involved with the sport the lure of Ironman was nipping at me. I'm not sure why. But it was calling me. I thought for sure my wife would have no part of it, but she was supportive. So I did it, I signed up for the 2010 Lake Placid Ironman. Wow!

The reason this is such a big deal is because five years ago I couldn't run a single lap around the local high school track without stopping. Literally. Now I am signed up to be an Ironman. Getting sober is the hardest thing I have ever done. Ironman will be the second. My goal in doing this is to show other addicts and alcoholics that "Anything is Possible."

I am planning on documenting the next year of my life and hopefully publishing a book about my journey. My goal is half triathlon and half sobriety. I want to make people aware that there are other options in life.

I am neither a seasoned professional athlete nor a person without a family. There are no guarantees that I will finish the race. But I will be putting every last ounce of effort that I have into this race.

The reason for my letter is to see if you would be interested in sponsoring me or donating a Tri-bike to my cause. I know that you get thousands of letters each year from people asking for your charity. I don't want to leave anything to chance. I need every advantage I can to finish; I think your bike can really help me.

I can't promise you any podiums or awards. I can't promise I will make any magazine covers. I can't promise that my book with get published. What I can promise is that I am going to do everything that I can to accomplish this task and show other people with Alcohol or Drug problems that "Anything is Possible."

If you have any interest in helping me with my journey, I can be reached at the contact information below. Thank you in advance for your consideration.

Within a week, I had my first reply from Kestrel Bikes. Steve Harad had written me back and told me that his sponsorship program was open and that he would see what he could do. After anxiously waiting for several weeks, I received the following email:

> Hello Athlete,
>
> Thank you for submitting your resume to be considered for the 2010 Kestrel Team. The response was overwhelming as we received many worthy resumes. At this time, I am happy to announce that *you have been chosen to represent the Kestrel Team in 2010!* Please read this letter carefully as it outlines what your Kestrel sponsorship entails.

I was ecstatic. Here I was a drunken bum of a human a few years ago, and now I was a sponsored athlete. Gadzooks! I sent the email to my wife and my buddy, John. I couldn't believe it, me, sponsored. They were just as thrilled as I was, mostly for me. I had asked my buddy if it was okay for me to write sponsor letters, and he told me yes. All I could do was ask, and the worst they could say was no. So I did. What made it even better was that Kestrel was based in Philly. I loved being associated with a company from my hometown.

What happened next was even more amazing—I got more. I was contacted by BlueSeventy and offered a sponsorship for their wetsuits. I was contacted by Speedplay pedals and offered a sponsorship with them. I started getting responses from all sorts of companies. Betsy Delcour contacted me from FuelBelt. She used to live around the corner from me and now lived in Denver; she sent me a fuel belt. I received products from Headsweats. I got products from Endurance Aid. Adamo saddles hooked me up with a saddle, and Total Immersion added some DVDs. Even the companies that couldn't offer me actual sponsorship opportunities offered me a deal to buy something at their professional discount. Several of the wheel manufacturers called me and told me that they would sell me wheels at cost. Elite Bicycles in Philadelphia offered me a free bike fitting. I was blown away. Here were good people trying to help a guy like me. I knew that if this thing worked out in the end, it's a feel-good story, but the truth is, they have businesses to run. They didn't have to help me, but they did. They took the time out of their day to help me. There are still good people in the world! Because of them, I will spend the rest of my life promoting their products and services to everyone I know.

Wow, Sponsored, Me!

I do have to admit that once I received the first sponsorship from Kestrel it put a bit more panic in me. My quest was, for all intents and purposes, flying under the radar to the rest of the world. Not anymore; now there were people who were going to know about me, and I was going to have to give pictures and updates. It's a bit overwhelming to go from a drunk who can't run to a sponsored athlete. Not that they were putting me on the cover of *Triathlete Magazine* or the "Tonight Show," but I still felt a responsibility to not let them down. I *had* to do this! I was willing to ask questions from anyone, anywhere, and put one foot in front of the other. If I was willing to do the work, adjust as I went, and ride the waves, both up and down, I knew I could do it.

TRAINING—PART 1

Now that I was signed up and in a full panic, I had to come up with yet another race plan. Keeping in mind the thirty different mistakes I had made in all of my previous races, I was pretty nervous about doing this one, especially since I now had some sponsors.

I had ordered a book the previous year called *BeIronFit* by Don Fink. I think when I originally ordered it I was just looking for a book about triathlons. I remember getting it and being disappointed because at the time, I hadn't really set my sights on doing an Ironman, so a lot of the book wasn't for me. In hindsight, he had a lot of tips that could be applied to any triathlon.

Once I had signed up and gotten some sponsors, I knew I needed a plan. I had done some research on beginnertriathlete. com and several people had recommended Don's book. So I went down to the basement and dusted it off. It had three different thirty-week training programs: Competitive, Just-Finish, and Intermediate. I read through each one and decided to go with intermediate. My thought was that if I could complete the intermediate training program it would allow me to "Just-Finish" easier. Not sure if that makes any sense or not, but it did to me at the time. I was trying to eliminate any possible reason for failure.

One of the things that I constantly struggled with in sobriety was my own brain. As some of us often say in sobriety, I don't have a drinking problem, I have a thinking problem. That was true for me. I spend a lot of time in my own head. Being an alcoholic inherently makes me want to isolate. Isolating makes me my only advisor. Not the best combination.

While I was getting better physically and emotionally every day, I was still far from "fixed." I questioned and re-questioned every decision I made. In triathlon and in life. There were times where I had read so much that my brain couldn't process it. I would go to the gym to exercise but didn't know what I wanted to do. I would literally just stand in the middle of the gym debating with myself for ten minutes.

Around then I was having lunch with my dad and doing my usual complaining about how messed up I thought I still was. I asked him why everyone else I saw looked like they had it together. He simply looked at me and said, "They're all full of crap." Apparently that had never occurred to me. For some reason I just assumed that the people who looked like they had it together actually did. Here I was trying to live up to a false ideal that my brain had created. It would tear me up inside to think how everyone else was so normal and that I was such a disaster.

I've since found out it is usually the opposite. If someone looks like they have everything figured out and all of their ducks lined up on the outside, they usually don't. They are usually an emotional, moral, or spiritual wreck.

I was still struggling with how I felt and what my brain was saying, but it helped to know that I was on the right path.

It was around August when I had decided on a plan. I pulled out the calendar and counted backward from the date of Ironman Lake Placid. My official training was to start on December 26, the day after Christmas. Ouch!

It's interesting how the human mind works. At the time, I had progressively gotten less and less worried about finishing the race. I knew that there were no guarantees, but if I stayed healthy and fed myself properly, I thought I would finish. Part of it is that you become more confident in your ability during training; the other part is that you become numb to the fear of it. Like anything else, we become complacent and forget. That was not how I felt after the sponsorship ordeal. I was really nervous and wanted to do anything I could to make sure I finished.

Being scared out of my mind that I had now officially signed up for the Ironman, I started to think about it all day long. What do I need? What should I do? Where do I stay? It was exhausting. For some reason, there is a certain amount of pressure that you put on yourself when you sign up for one of these. You almost feel like you have some nerve even attempting an Ironman, so you better back it up. I know, macho bull! The other thing I kept thinking was that my family was going to have to put up with a lot for over a half a year, so I'd better finish and make it worth their while. I also couldn't stop thinking about my father telling half of his buddies that "My son is doing an Ironman." I didn't want to let him down. Even though I was doing the race for myself, I didn't want to let any of them down.

Since the very beginning, I had prescribed to one main philosophy that I hoped would get me through this. That philosophy being "With every step forward, I am one step closer to the end. Just keep taking steps forward." I used this a lot!

The other thing that I think really helped me early on was a quote by a woman on beginnertriathlete.com, which said, "Rarely is my ability to perform physical." That was me. I knew going in, I was going to need to get stronger mentally. Again, physically talented, mentally not so much. I could hit a golf ball from here to New Jersey but just didn't care. I needed to get stronger mentally.

One of the other things I struggled with on and off during my recovery was my spirituality. Physically, emotionally, and spiritually bankrupt was how I entered into sobriety. I was working on the physical and emotional part, but spirituality was coming to me slowly. Part of the reason was that I went through sixteen years of Catholic school. So much of my thought patterns were ingrained in me. Part of it was that I was born with a logical head. To complicate things over the years, I had read books on Buddhism, Taoism, the Bible and the like. What this created was a giant cauldron of information that my mind was not ready to handle. I could go from telling you why the Bible made no sense to arguing with you about the perfection of the universe and who must have created it.

It was around this time in my training that I realized that I needed to be stronger spiritually. I couldn't do this on my own. I needed help from the man upstairs, even if I didn't have an official definition of him yet. I knew I was going to have to be as centered and grounded as possible. I couldn't do it on my own.

For those of you who aren't in recovery, I'll sum this up for you with the following, "There is something out there controlling the universe, and it ain't me." I needed all the help I could get. I was going to use every tool I could. To me, being spiritually centered was just as important as any of them. I needed to be right mentally, physically, and spiritually if I was going to finish this race. I was not going to leave any stone unturned.

Much like the previous triathlons I had done, I decided that I didn't want day one of my training to be day one of my training. Anyone who has ever exercised or skied after not doing it for a while knows how much you can hurt the next few days. I didn't want that to be me, so I started running and sporadically lifting weights almost immediately after I signed up for the Ironman.

When I had first started training, I thought it might be a good idea to keep a journal. I don't know if I thought I would actually write a book or if I just wanted it for my own personal development. Either way, I started writing stuff down on August 17, 2009. On August 18, I realized it was going to be a long ride…

Here are my first two entries:

8/17/09

Did a 73 minute run at Wissahickon Park today. Weather would have been great if I had gotten up early, but I was wiped from going to the pool the day before with some friends. I got there around 10:00 a.m. and started my run. This was my first run of any length since the OLY two weeks ago. I had planned on running in Paris (where I took my wife for our anniversary), but we were walking so much every day I thought it would do more harm than good.

I felt good throughout the run. I took my time, didn't go too fast. This was also the first time that I wore a hydration belt. I filled it with Heed. My goal over the next 6 months is to experiment with all of the nutrition. After my last race where I ate too much on the bike and my stomach was doing back flips on the run, I want to make sure I listen to people and actually do the experimenting during training. In this case I used power bar refueling powder and mixed it up with some water. I made sure that I drank some every 20 minutes. I also stopped at a water fountain twice. The run felt great. I don't know if it's because my legs were rested or I was fueling right or both. But it was nice to get a positive run under my belt.

I can do this!

8/18/09

It's amazing how the human brain works sometimes. I'm in LA this morning traveling on business. It 6:16 local time and I just finished my workout. Was on the bike for an hour. (I hate sit down bikes. They don't make sit down stair steppers.) After about the first 20 minutes I was feeling good. Looking at myself, I was feeling great. Legs felt good, lungs, the whole thing. I have IM in my sights and it's pumping me up. Then I made the mistake of opening a book I was reading on Ironman. The guy was talking about time goals. He was talking about whether you were looking to finish or hit a certain goal. Then I saw it:

Lake Placid Ironman
Swim – 1:05
Bike – 5:45
Run – 4:09

This was 11:00 hours. For some reason this scared the crap out of me. I couldn't do a 4 hour marathon on roller skates rolling down from Mt. Everest. I was planning at least 6. I don't really have any idea how long the bike will take yet, but that seems fast. And the swim. I just did the New Jersey State Olympic and did the mile swim in 39 minutes. 1:05 is only 26 minutes faster than that to do 1.4 times more distance.

What the hell was I thinking signing up for this? As always, I will try to ignore the thoughts and just keep moving forward. With each step I move closer to the goal and further from the start.

As you can see, it didn't take long for me to jump onto an emotional roller coaster. I was only in the first couple of weeks, and already I had two different days with two different levels of confidence. This would be indicative of the next eleven months of my life. I was either feeling good or panicking. I had a fair amount of days in between, but I don't know if I can take credit for them or if I was just numb to the whole thing.

I spent the next few months struggling, trying to figure out what to do with my training. My race wasn't until the end of July, and it was only September. In typical fashion, I confused myself. *Should I really train hard so the Ironman training is easier? Should I run a marathon? Should I do a half-Ironman, which I am not really prepared for? Should I just sign up for an Olympic, even though I am not ready just to get some training for my head? Should I just lift heavy weights with my legs to bulk them up? What should I do?*

I literally spent hours thinking about this. Again, I have to give some credit to beginnertriathlete.com. Discovering that site really helped me get through most of my triathlons. It's a great site with all kinds of information. You can go on the forums and ask any kind of question that you want, and someone will have had some experience with it.

One of my first thoughts was that I should run a marathon. After all, *I have to run a marathon in the Ironman,* I thought, and since running is my biggest weakness, this would give me some confidence and have me go through the mental part of 26.2 miles. I can honestly say I think the responses on the forum were pretty much down the middle. Some people said it was a great idea; others said it was pointless. They had as many reasons as I have fingers and toes. The one that stuck with me the most and ultimately made my decision for me was from a person who said the following, "You don't run the marathon portion of an Ironman. You simply keep yourself moving forward, it's totally different than running a marathon."

As with many other things, that one hit me for some reason. Combined with the fact that I wasn't sure if I could actually run the marathon and then recover fast enough to start my training in December, I decided against it.

Woo hoo! I don't have to do a marathon. (I really don't love running so much.)

But what should I be doing? I thought about starting the Ironman training program earlier, and then a bunch of people told me that I will be so sick of the Ironman training part that I shouldn't prolong it anymore than it needed to be. They, however, didn't have any sponsors and an alcoholic brain that makes everything worse than it really is.

So should I stop all together? If I do that, then I think my aerobic base will suffer, and I will have a hard time the first couple of months of my IM training.

I went back and forth and back and forth over and over. For those people that thought I was this great athlete with tremendous willpower, think again. I'm a regular Joe with regular thoughts, about ten thousand too many of them per day.

I was starting to make myself sick. I had fifty different suggestions and fifty different ideas. The truth is that I still didn't know what to do. But I kept doing something, whether it was a rowing machine or stair stepper; I made sure I was doing some form of exercise.

In the end, I had pretty much decided to work on my weaknesses, strength train, and have at least one long run a week. If I needed to be moving for 140.6 miles, I would need all the help I could get.

When I first started figuring out my training program, I was about 215 pounds. I had made a completely uneducated decision that I needed to get down to 185-190 before the race. I haven't been 185 since I was twenty. I had done the Body for Life program before with my wife after my daughter Emily was born. I liked it. I am kind of a weight lifting, protein shake type of guy anyway. So I decided to do that for the ninety days leading up to December 26th. This would give me some structure and would hopefully get me down to a good weight. It would also build some muscle for me, especially in my legs. (I have chicken legs.)

The Body for Life program worked well for me, and I still had the desire and drive to get up at 5:15 a.m. every day to go to the gym. Of course, I could still wear shorts to the gym and was still excited to be training for something. I have always liked lifting weights, and the longest cardio sessions I was doing at that time were thirty minutes. But if you are like me, you quickly realize that it's not the beginning of your training that matters; it's the end. Starting something is not all that impressive; finishing it is what's important. I would find that out in just about every way during my training.

I did well for those first three months. I followed the rigorous diet and hit the gym six days a week. For those of you who have never tried the Body for Life program, I would recommend it. You actually have to eat a lot of food (good food) and don't have to kill yourself with exercise. Of the six days, you may exercise for an hour two of those days. The rest are usually half an hour or less. I can do that. I can do weight lifting and treadmill for short periods of time fairly easily.

I had no major roadblocks with the diet part. The nice thing about Body for Life is that they have you eat a ton of food to jump-start your metabolism. So I can honestly say that I was never hungry. On top of that, I got to eat whatever I wanted on the seventh day (cheat day), so it made it all worthwhile.

Those first three months went by so quickly. I was still jacked up about having signed up for the Ironman, and the sponsorship pressure that I had put on myself had died down a bit. I was getting up early, losing weight, and feeling good.

Just after Thanksgiving, I had gone to work like any other day. A woman that I worked with who knew my cousin Joe said to me, "Sorry to hear about your cousin."

I said, "What about him?"

She said, "Oh, I'm sorry. I thought you knew. His son has leukemia."

I was devastated. While Joe is not my brother, I always felt like he was. We had a special connection in my mind. Not only did we party together; he was my confirmation sponsor when I was in grade school, and I wanted to be just like him when I grew up. As fate would have it, we ended up being a lot alike and spending a lot of time together over the years. He had cleaned himself up and started a new family. Now his son was sick.

I spent the rest of that day completely numb. As much as I tried, I couldn't move out of total shock. I just couldn't believe it. How could this happen? Why him? Why Joe? Why did he have to go through this?

I went home that night and told my wife and proceeded to go up to our bedroom to lie down. When my wife finally came up and sat with me, I broke down. I hugged her and cried my eyes out for a half an hour. I can honestly say that I can't remember being that upset in a long time.

I'm not sure if it was because I loved him like a brother or because I had a daughter the same age as his son or a combination of both, but it felt like someone had kicked me in the stomach. All of the sudden, my tiny, little Ironman didn't seem to matter. In the grand scheme of things, it was irrelevant.

That day was the closest that I had been to wanting to drink since my first year sober. I hadn't felt like drinking in a long time. It certainly wasn't because I was cured. It was mostly because I had been given tools to use. Picking up the phone and talking to another alcoholic. Having coffee with another alcoholic. Trying to help someone new get sober. These were all ways to help me stay sober. I was so numb that whole day and in such shock I didn't know how to deal with it.

As I was taught, I got myself up the next morning to go meet my friend John for coffee. I told him about my cousin, and we talked through the whole thing. He was the one who first pointed out that I might be upset because my daughter was the same age.

Nevertheless, we talked it out, and I felt better. Another lesson I learn from being an alcoholic, talk to someone about it; it will make you feel better.

Later that day, my cousin called me back. He was doing okay. He was upset but hopeful. His son was at Children's Hospital of Philadelphia, which is one of the best children's hospitals in the country. He was going to get the best care available.

Having gotten sober a few years before me, Joe also had a great support system around him. He had people to talk to and shoulders to cry on. He didn't have to go through it alone. He also had five brothers and sisters and a pretty tight family.

It made me feel better to talk to him. He was upset, but he was handling it. He had a great support structure and a strong faith.

The first couple of weeks after Thanksgiving, I remained numb. I continued my exercise and diet program to help me get through it. I knew how I felt. I couldn't even imagine myself going through something that difficult. I often look at people who go through tough things like that and am amazed. I really don't know if I could be that strong. I have other friends whose kids are in rehab and are in trouble with the law, and they handle it. I can only hope I could be so strong.

As with anything, the numbness wore off over time.

The Body for Life program finished for me right around Christmas. I was happy to be done with it, in some respects, even though I felt better. My starting weight was 215, and I tipped the scales at 200 on my last day. At two hundred pounds, I was in good shape, muscular, almost ripped. I wasn't really sure if I could get to 185 or not. I knew muscle weighted more than fat, but I didn't know if it weighed that much. Maybe two hundred pounds was the right weight for someone like me that was built like a tight end.

As Christmas crept up, the whole family was on board with my Ironman. Despite me spending all of my time on triathlon websites and constantly ordering stuff, all of my gifts were triathlon-related; from socks to towels to hats to sunscreen. Even my wife was now rifling through my triathlon magazines and finding things that I needed.

It had been an emotional first three months, from my cousin's son being sick to creating my own anxiety I had been all over the map. I was about to enter that real part of my training and see what kind of mettle I really had.

Training—Part 2

I wrote at the beginning of this book that I had twelve failed diets during my Ironman training. It could have just as easily been fifty. Part of it is having this crazy head that goes back and forth on what is best for me, and part of it is that I am extremely good at rationalizing everything.

I had done well with Body for Life, but that was now behind me. Now I was doing full-blown cardio at least six days a week and wasn't really sure how to eat. I had bought three different diet books for endurance athletes, and none of them helped me. It wasn't the books, I just don't really have any interest in making my food consumption a game of biology and chemistry. Most of them had scientific formulas and measurements and watts put out by the body and blah blah blah. That's too much for me to follow. Just tell me what to eat and when, and I will do it. That's why I do well with Body for Life. If it's a full-time job, then forget it.

So within the first week or two of my actual Ironman training, I was without a diet. Now that I was about six months removed from signing up for the race, the impending doom of it wasn't as strong. Plus, I had decided that if I was going to be burning a million calories per week exercising, why couldn't I just eat whatever I wanted? Seemed to make sense to me, so that's what I did.

As with all of my training to date, the Ironman program started off fairly mild. I biked two days a week, ran two days, and swam three days. Much like the diet, I needed someone to tell me exactly what to do and when, and that's exactly what *BeIronFit* did.

If you are like me and live in the Northeastern part of the country, winter can be a dark and depressing time of year. I used to have an office in the center of my building that had no windows. During especially busy days, I would put my head down and work and when I left, it was already dark. Combine that with getting up at 5:00 a.m. and getting in the pool, and you swear you haven't seen light in months. It took me a long time as an adult to realize it, but I really do suffer from depression during those months of the year.

Things had gone fine the first few weeks of training. I was still pumped up enough to be excited about training, and the record Philly snowfall hadn't really started yet.

The job I had was perfect for my Ironman training. It was a job that I had been doing for five years. I was the director at a medical software company in Philadelphia. I could do that job with my eyes closed. When you are thinking about signing up for an Ironman, you think of all the different things that will go into your success. How supportive will my spouse be? Will I still be around for my kids? Does my job afford me the time that I need? I had thought about each of these things prior to signing up and was convinced that I could do it.

A few weeks into the New Year, I got a somewhat disturbing message from the CEO's office. He wanted to see me at 4:00 p.m. It was a Friday.

Being the half class-clown person that I am, I proceeded to ask if I was going to need a flak jacket. I was told no but the CEO wanted to meet me alone.

In all honesty, I wasn't really worried that I was going to get fired but I would be lying if I said the thought hadn't crossed my mind. In hindsight, it probably wouldn't have been the worst thing if I had.

I walked into the CEO's office at 3:59. He closed the door, and we sat down across from each other at a small table in his office. He went through a five-minute dissertation about my success record with the company and how many good references I had. He proceeded to tell me how much I was respected by my peers and presidents throughout the company.

Then he said, "I'd like you to run the sales division for the eastern US."

He followed that up by telling me that he had done some research and hadn't realized how much sales experience I had. He also told me he was going to make me an offer that I couldn't refuse.

Then, in Hollywood fashion, he took a piece of paper out of his pocket, put it on the table, and slid it across to me. When I unfolded it, it said three things: My current salary, what my new salary would be, and the percentage increase.

I looked at the piece of paper for a minute then gave him some of my thoughts. I told him that I had some specific concerns and that I would appreciate the opportunity to discuss this opportunity with my wife over the weekend, to which he agreed. I left his office with a smile on my face. It's amazing how your emotions can rollercoaster on you and how fast.

When I got back to my office, I called my wife and told her that we were going out for sushi. "We needed to discuss something."

One of the few compliments I will actually give myself is that I am pretty levelheaded. I don't just jump at things that are right in front of me without thinking them through. In fact, about two years prior to this, I was offered the same job, which I promptly turned down. That time, of course, I wasn't asked by the CEO.

The raise was significant enough that it would have made anyone think about it. But a raise isn't the end of the world, and if you are set up to fail, it may do more harm than good in the long run.

So I drove myself crazy for the next forty-eight hours. I had to have an answer by 8:00 a.m. Monday morning, and I honestly didn't know what to do.

The job itself was a bit more than I probably wanted. I liked sales and liked dealing with customers, but this was a lot more than that. This job involved me completely rebuilding, retraining, and re-staffing an entire sales department. That involved firing a few people, moving some people around, and ultimately hiring eight people to replace the attrition that had happened over the past few years.

While I was okay with all of those things, I had some concerns that the person who had caused most of the current problems was still with the company. Corporate America is really scary sometimes.

In the end, I decided to talk to the CEO about what I felt the issues would be. He assured me that he had an open door, and we shook on our new deal.

While the salary increase of this new job came as a welcome surprise, the new responsibility and amount of work that I now had to do was staggering. I went from having a job that I could do with my eyes closed to spending my evenings at home on the couch reading resumes. I was to have a team of eleven people. Three were currently on the payroll. Two of those were being reassigned.

My new job could have just as easily been called human resources recruiter/trainer. I estimate that I looked at over a thousand resumes and interviewed scores of people. To add insult to injury, I was flying all around the country to do it. So not only was I working a lot, but I was doing a lot of it from a hotel.

Looking back on it, it was a lot, but it happened at the right time. The first three months of the year were the lightest part of my training. Had it been in the second or third part, I don't know if I would be sitting here writing this.

I spent the better part of my first three months of Ironman training working, interviewing, and training. The training had not yet gotten to a point where it was unbearable, and the job was actually making the days go fast.

The most difficult thing about training with a job like mine is the travel. At home, it's easy. Even though the kids have soccer games and dance class, you're in your comfort zone. You know what the gym hours are, and you always have a car. When you travel, you may or may not even been in an area that has a gym, let alone a pool. Oftentimes, you take taxis from the airport to the hotel and don't have a car.

Like anything else in life, you learn to adapt. You start calling the hotel ahead of time to see if they have a gym. If you need to swim on a particular day, you find out if the hotel is near a YMCA or gym with a pool. If you need to run a particular day, you ask local people if there is a good running trail. I didn't always get the best solutions, but I made do. As usual, there were solutions if you looked for them. It would have been easy for me to give up, but I didn't. I made it work.

What made matters worse for me during those first few months was how rigid I was with my training. I never missed a workout! Literally. It didn't matter if I had to go to the pool at ten o'clock at night; I went. If my plane got in late and I couldn't run, I added it to the next day's workout. At the time, I was convinced that it was like a priest missing mass on Sunday. In my mind, if I missed even one workout, I was putting myself at the risk of not finishing the race. So I did what any good alcoholic would do; I went to the other extreme.

I will say that many of the things that happened from a job perspective during those first three to four months were my choice. We had an outside recruiter that I didn't like, so I recruited all of the people myself with the help of our internal HR staff. HR had other people they needed to hire, and I didn't have time to wait, so I did most of the screening myself. I knew how to sell our products better than most people in the building, so I did all the training myself. I wasn't a big fan of the training we had been giving these reps for years, and I chose now as the time to fix it.

When it was all said and done, it was a lot of work, but it got done. I did everything I needed to do at work and didn't miss a workout. That included trips to Hershey, Pennsylvania; Huntingdon, West Virginia; Columbus, Ohio; Birmingham, Alabama; Greensboro, North Carolina; Nashville, Tennessee; Hartford, Connecticut; Orlando, Florida; and Miami, twice.

The first time I felt a chink in the armor was probably March. While I was getting all my work done and the workouts were moving along, it was around then that the volume of training increased. It was now to the point that during three of the four weekdays that I trained, the training was such that I couldn't complete it all in one session. If you have to run for an hour and swim for an hour with time in between and traffic, it's almost impossible to do it all before work. If you had to do it after the kids went to sleep, you were rushing to get it done before they turned the lights out at the gym.

So now I was doing two training sessions per day three times per week, one in the morning, one whenever I could fit it in. Sometimes I would race over to the gym at lunch, while other times I puttered in at nine o'clock at night. Either way, I got them done.

At the beginning, I was religious about getting up and knocking out the first one right away. But as the cold and snow keeps coming, it zaps the life out of you.

Eventually, I found yet another solution. I joined a second gym. While my main gym has the pool and is close to my house, the other gym was literally next door to my work. I could walk over there during lunch and bike or run for an hour and be back at work before anyone knew I was gone. It was perfect.

Another challenge, another solution.

Despite all of the insanity that was going on, I was handling it pretty well. I felt good physically, and the training hadn't yet kicked my butt. I had so much going on I didn't even have time to think about drinking. In fact, from a sobriety standpoint I was doing a lousy job. I wasn't doing my best to keep up with my sober friends or doing any of the things that I had learned. I was skating by. Lucky for me, I was so busy it didn't matter.

One of the things that *BeIronFit* had me do was to sign up for some practice races. Part of it is to practice physically, the other to practice transitions and the mental part. I had signed up for a half-Ironman in Connecticut and an Olympic tri in New Jersey. It was the Olympic where I would first start to question myself and my motives.

THE BASSMAN OLYMPIC TRIATHLON

My training up to this point had gone reasonably well. Despite increasing bouts of exhaustion, I was still moving forward. I was starting to get a bit sick of the training but mostly from a mental standpoint. I didn't mind exercising; it was the fact that I always felt like I "had" to. If I wanted to come home and just relax, I couldn't; I had to run. If I wanted to get up on Saturday and go to a baseball game, I couldn't; I had to bike. It gets somewhat overwhelming, but at this point, I was still okay.

The Bassman Olympic Triathlon was the closest thing I could find that fit into my training schedule. It was in New Jersey and was probably about an hour-and-a-half from my house.

I had done the training for an Olympic distance race when I did the New Jersey State tri, but now I was training for an Ironman. My swimming was stronger, my biking was better, and I had been running a lot. I fully expected to crush this race. This was aerobically the best shape I had ever been in so far in my life.

Since most triathlons start at some ungodly hour, and I have a problem with being early, I decided to stay at my parents' house in Cape May, New Jersey. This would put me about a half hour away from the race, so I wouldn't have to get up at three thirty in the morning to get there.

As usual, I got up too early and was getting coffee before the night manager finished his shift. Being at the Jersey Shore off season is a not a far cry from being in *Deliverance*. There are some odd people that lurk about in the daylight, let alone at 5:00 a.m.

Once I had enough caffeine for my trip, I hit the road and began my journey. Unlike the Philadelphia and New Jersey tris, this was much smaller. You couldn't just follow all the cars and get to where you needed to be. It was also in the middle of a densely wooded park. Not only was it in the middle of a park, it was in the middle of a park that wasn't well marked. Combine that with the New Jersey Pine Barrens, and you get the picture.

I followed the same pattern for this race as I had for all of my previous races. I got there first. Apparently, they don't give out trophies for people who get to the parking lot first. This seemed to be the only thing I was actually fast at.

Once I got there, I did my thing, got marked up, put my bike in transition, and got myself situated. One of the things that had happened over the past few months was that I got a sponsorship deal with BlueSeventy. So in addition to getting myself some new goggles, I got a brand spanking new Helix wetsuit.

Right out of the box, this wetsuit was nicer than the one I had before. It was more tailored and not just one big piece of rubber. Being the thickheaded nimrod that I am, I, of course, tried it on at home but didn't swim in it yet. In this case, I felt okay about it because the previous four months had been winter, and I simply didn't have the chance. Nevertheless, I hadn't worn it swimming in the water. You would think that almost drowning twice would have taught me something.

For whatever reason, I wasn't as worried as I was before. Maybe it was because we weren't in a huge city river but a pond at the park. Maybe it was because the race director told us that you could basically touch the ground the whole way around. Whatever it was, I was fine mentally. I got in the water before the race and did a small practice swim. The water was cold, really cold. Usually, it takes water some time to catch up with the outside temperature, and it was only May. I don't know what the temperature was, but if you swam without a wetsuit, I'll bet you had a good chance at hypothermia. So any chance in my mind of swimming without the wetsuit was soon extinguished.

Nothing out of the ordinary happened during the practice swim.

After that, I did what was now my standard pacing before the race. I walked back and forth and back and forth, never really getting anywhere or accomplishing anything. I'm not sure if that is from nerves or not wanting to talk to anyone, but I can't sit still.

Eventually, the race began. Wave after wave of people jumped in the water, while I stood and watched. Once my wave came up, we all hopped into the water. Quickly, we all started to splash and slosh our way out to a depth where we could swim. Having learned my lesson, I started out slow and let all the kamikazes go in front of me.

The cold water hit me harder than I thought it would. Even though I had done a warm-up, it was making it hard to breathe. If you've ever gotten into a really cold pool, you know what that feels like. Combined with the fact that I was wearing a wetsuit, I fell right back into my pattern of not being able to swim. I made it about thirty yards before it hit me. I couldn't breathe. No matter what I did, it just wasn't working. However, unlike the last time, I could actually just stop swimming and float. With the previous wetsuit and a full running river, I was forced to grab onto a kayak. This time, I could just stop until I caught my breath then try again, each time hyperventilating as soon as my face hit the frigid water. I was convinced it wasn't the suit; it was the temperature of the water this time. I was pissed. I had spent all of this time in the pool. I had changed wetsuits. I was getting angrier and angrier with each yard I swam.

Eventually, I was forced into what can only be described as a doggie paddle. I half propelled myself across the bottom with my feet and half doggie paddled.

In the end, I was one of the last people out of the water. I was so furious that I again considered quitting races all together. It probably took me at least double the amount of time that I had anticipated.

Fortunately for me, this was the first race with my new bike. I had gotten a Talon SL from my bike sponsor Kestrel. It was a rocket ship with wheels. It was super fast and light as a feather. Regardless of my swim, I was excited to get on the bike. Part of it was that I was looking forward to opening her up, and the other part was that I wanted to get away from the water as fast as possible.

The race director described the race as a flat race with great paved roads. I'm not sure where he grew up, but those roads were barely paved. On a mountain bike, you can drive across corncobs and not feel a thing; on a road bike, you can feel a paperclip in the road. If you've ever driven on a road where they remove the blacktop so that they can re-asphalt it, that's what the whole race felt like. I could have popped popcorn if you put some in my pants I was jerking around so much.

Despite the not so great road conditions and the general lack of any direction whatsoever on the course itself, the bike route wasn't terrible.

What killed us all was the pollen.

Keep in mind that we were essentially riding through what are called the New Jersey Pine Barrens. If you aren't familiar with the Pine Barrens, it is basically a forest of pine trees that stretches from Southern New Jersey all the way up to New York. It can be dense in some areas and right next to the highway in others. We were riding right through the center of it for this race.

I have spent a lot of my life outside, from being on my bike as a kid to working outside at a golf course in college. I had never seen anything like this. The pollen from these trees was literally blowing in your face in clouds of dust. To put this in perspective, I wore black tri shorts and a mostly black and yellow Livestrong shirt. If you saw me when I got off the bike from over ten yards away, you would have thought I wore a completely yellow outfit. I was literally yellow from head to toe. It was as if the local grade school had all of their classes go outside and clap their erasers at the same time.

If the wind blew, forget about it. You literally had to turn your head away or cover your mouth. We were all hacking and coughing the whole ride. It was impossible to ever really catch your breath.

Despite the insanity of the pollen, I actually did okay on the bike. I passed a lot of people and was flying on my new bike. While I probably inhaled a few pounds of pollen, I felt fine when I finally got off the bike.

As was becoming an all-too-familiar site, there were more bikes back in transition than not. I know that I am 205 pounds, but it can still get a bit frustrating at times. In most sporting events, being big is an advantage, not so much in endurance sports.

Even though I had spent too much time and energy in the water and had caked my lungs with pollen, I still felt okay when I got off the bike. That was a feeling that quickly went away when I started the run. I ran about a half a mile before I had to stop. I couldn't breathe, my legs hurt, and I was getting cramps. Again, I was pissed. Why was this happening? *I've trained so hard; this should be easy,* I thought. But it wasn't. I struggled with every step I took. I'm not sure if I am just a slow runner or I expended too much energy in the previous two disciplines. Whatever it was, it was getting frustrating, and fast.

And that wasn't even the worst part.

I managed to run for another mile or so. I was still hurting but was moving myself forward. I had come up to a part in the road where it merged with another road. As I was running, I could see out of the corner of my eye that there were some people running through the woods on my right side about thirty yards away, heading for the same place I was. *Where are they going? What are they doing?* I thought. When it was one person, I thought maybe he needed a bathroom break. When I saw ten, I knew I was in trouble.

Holy crap, I missed a turn!

While it was not the best organized event I have ever been at, I'm sure there was a sign that told me I was supposed to turn. I missed the turn. That turn was an extra 1.5 miles that I had just short-cut my way through. I didn't do it on purpose, but now I was completely disgusted. It was too far to go back and now that I missed it, I would probably be disqualified for not crossing the mat with my timing chip.

We all merged together and kept running. I went from being upset that I was racing so poorly to being downright ready to quit. I started to question why I was doing all of this. *Why was I doing triathlons? This is a little man's sport. Who do I think I am?* I spent the remaining miles of the run suffering physically and mentally, telling myself that I couldn't do this and that I didn't belong here.

By the time I finished the race, I was spent. I had a lousy race and wanted no part of triathlons anymore. Why does a big slow goof like me need a $3,000 bike anyway? Looking around transition, I saw nothing but smiles. Everyone was happy and comparing their times. I didn't want to talk to any of them; I just wanted to get my things and go.

Embarrassed, I packed my stuff up as fast as I could and hit the road.

It was a long two-hour drive home.

Training—Part 3

I was really depressed after the race in New Jersey. I really thought that I was going to knock 'em dead. Instead, I turned in one of the worst performances I could have imagined. What made matters worse was that I had no idea why. I had done all of the training and thought I was ready, but that race had clearly beaten me. How the hell was I ever going to do an Ironman?

My alcoholism really came out as soon as I got in the car to drive home. I was angry, tired, and frustrated. I was full of fear and self-doubt. The looming embarrassment that I felt put me over the top. I starting questioning everything from why I was doing this to who I thought I was to even try. I went downhill hard and fast.

Being a dry drunk is no picnic. While I wasn't putting any alcohol in my body, I could still stomp my feet and act like a child. That's exactly what I was doing. Although I wasn't drinking, I hadn't been keeping up with my sobriety, and it got the better of me.

My overall depression lasted for about a week. I can't accurately describe how much I actually wanted to quit this whole journey. It really knocked the life out of me. I think I again told my wife that I wanted to quit, and she again told me I wasn't allowed. I sulked and screamed and whined for the whole week, mostly to myself.

Once the dust settled, I knew I had to keep going. I would regret it for the rest of my life if I didn't. Plus, I had a half-Ironman coming up in another month or so, and I didn't want to have the same experience there.

I got back into my training the following week but wasn't really all that happy about it. Either way, I was committed to putting one foot in front of the other, so I did it.

I spent the next several weeks researching nutrition. While my nutrition plan was better than the one I had for the New Jersey State tri, it was far from what it needed to be.

I, of course, came from the era where "hydration" was not that big of a deal. You played football, baseball, and hockey all day, and never once did you carry your own bottled water.

Today, fueling your body is its own science, from how many calories your body can absorb to how much water you should consume to how much salt you need to replace. You almost need a degree in chemistry just to figure out what you should use for your races and in training. To make matters worse, add heat, course elevation, and length if you really want to mix things up. Did you know you can actually die from drinking too much water? Who ever heard of such a thing?

It didn't take me long to figure out that there were five hundred different variations on nutrition. What's funny about them is that every company swears that theirs is the right way. They all have scientific research, and they all have their little charts. If you are like me, you end up more confused than when you started.

I had done enough research online and from all the books that I bought that I had made one good decision. I wanted a single product. What that meant to me was that I could buy a powder, mix it with the correct amount of water, and that was it. I didn't have to take any salt pills or eat additional calories.

I decided on Infinit Nutrition. It had everything I felt I needed—calories, carbs, caffeine, and salt. And it was easy to use. Some of the other brands that were out there had you bringing five different bags of stuff with you, and I just didn't have time for that.

Learning about nutrition was a very important step. While I may not have realized it when I started, I certainly did by the time I was finished. What I didn't know was that most of the people who drop out of an Ironman drop out because of gastrointestinal issues. I had always thought people dropped out because they just couldn't do it, but that's not the case. They either fuel their body too much and the stomach can't absorb the calories and it just sits there (like in my New Jersey State race), or they don't fuel enough and run out of energy. It is not an exact science and is somewhat of a moving target.

Over the next few weeks, I was starting to grow weary of all of the training. I had been training nonstop for about eight months straight with little if any time off. Combined with the fact that I had some lingering depression from my most recent race, I was becoming more and more miserable about having to train.

Not long after the Bassman race, I had lost all motivation. I was upset about how bad I did and was just plain tired. I went onto begginertriathlete.com and posted the following message:

> This is hard for me to admit, but I have to be honest, I am losing my motivation. Four months into my Training for LP I am starting to get a bit tired of it. In the beginning I was jumping out of bed at 5:00 a.m. to hit the swim. Now I sleep in and do my workouts at night and at lunch. I am just starting to lose the thrill of it all and can't figure out how to get it back. I am not going to quit; I have come too

far. I just need some help figuring out how to re-motivate myself. Any thoughts would be appreciated

People gave me all sorts or encouragement and suggestions. They ranged from watching the world championships on TV to doing a shorter race to taking some time off.

One of the mistakes I had made was that I spent the majority of the winter watching Ironman races on Universal sports. So when I needed the added motivation of seeing those shows, their effectiveness had worn off. I still enjoyed watching them, but they didn't help with my motivation.

Doing a shorter race was out of the question. I was still mad about the race I had just done. The chance of me blowing another race and having me really melt down was too great.

What I ended up doing was yet another life lesson. I took a week off.

Having been so rigid and so committed in the end actually hurt me. I was burned out from all the training. Not only mentally but physically. My body was tired. My brain was tired. I needed a rest, and I was too hardheaded to see it. Despite having read two hundred articles telling me to listen to my body, I forced myself to continue. I can't imagine what would have happened had I not taken the break.

A week later, I was back. I felt better mentally and physically. In hindsight, I had read enough articles about beginners overtraining that I should have known better, but the weight of the Ironman on my shoulders made me keep trudging along.

A week on the couch had done me good. I had some much-needed rest and a renewed interest in my goal. While my enthusiasm was not the same as the day I signed up, it wasn't as bad as when I finished the Bassman either.

In the midst of all of this, my daughter's softball season started. To my dismay, I was to be the coach this year. I had signed up to be an assistant coach but somehow got the dreaded head coaching job instead. I wasn't upset about it because I didn't want to do it; it was more because of my busy travel schedule and the amount of upcoming training I had to do. After discussing these issues with my two assistant coaches, I reluctantly accepted the position.

I often do things that I dreaded the thought of doing, only to have it turn out better than I expected. That's what coaching softball was for me. Being an alcoholic and an isolator, I don't generally like dealing with whole groups of people, let alone being the one that they are all looking at. On top of that, I don't particularly like parents. We have all heard the stories about how crazy parents are with athletics, and I lived in a neighborhood full of them.

What happened during the course of the season is that I ended up loving it. I enjoyed talking to the little girls and telling them how to play the game. I had first and second graders, so the point was to teach them the game, not to be super competitive. We taught them how to hit and field and the basic rules of the game. I ended up loving every minute of it. I would sit at work and actually look forward to it. I remember standing on the pitcher's mound one day, wondering to myself how many other things in life that I thought I hated that maybe I would really like. We ended up having a pretty good group of girls who all progressively got better with each game. Mission accomplished!

The only downside to softball season was the fact that it was simply another thing for me to juggle with my schedule. Training and work were enough; anything I added to that mix just made it more difficult—difficult, not impossible.

I made my way through the month of May. Training was becoming harder and much longer, especially on the weekends. I was biking fifty to eighty-five miles on Saturday, followed by long runs on Sunday. While I was way stronger than I had ever been, it was still physically difficult at times, especially trying to do a two-hour run after biking seventy-five miles the day before.

Before I knew it, the half-Ironman I had signed up for was upon me. It's not as easy as you think to find the distance race you are looking for on a specific weekend in your backyard. The *BeIronFit* training had planned for me to do a half-Ironman about ten weeks before Ironman Lake Placid. There were none in Philly, none in Jersey, none in Delaware, and none in New York. The Rev3 Quassy in Middlebury, Connecticut, is where I ended up.

It was within driving distance of Philadelphia and boasted a star-studded lineup of top pros. Craig Alexander, who had won the last two Ironman World Championships, was there, along with a whole host of other top names in the sport.

The half-Ironman was something I was actually looking forward to. I still thought that I would be okay with the new wetsuit and now understood enough about nutrition to make me dangerous. I was well trained and felt good about my ability to not melt down again.

Rev3 holds an Olympic race on Saturday and the half-Iron distance on Sunday. Since it was a good three hours away, I needed to stay at a hotel the night before the race.

My original plan was to go up on Saturday night after having spent some time with the kids. Then I found out that I needed to be up there by 4:00 p.m. to pick up my race packet.

Being the insane person I am, I was on the road by 7:00 a.m. on Saturday. My reason was not triathlon-related; it was New York City-related. I had been in Connecticut twice in the previous few months, and the New York traffic killed me. I have lived within ninety miles of NYC my whole life; I know what the traffic is like. For some reason, the past two times I had to come home, I sat in traffic waiting to get over that stupid George Washington Bridge for hours.

I made a decision that I was not going to do that this time. And I didn't. I left my house at 7:00 a.m. and was passing NYC shortly after eight. It was so early, in fact, that I got to Connecticut in record time, 2.5 hours. While that is great time, it doesn't actually work out well when you can't check into your hotel until three and can't pick up your packet until 1:00 p.m. Classic John Toth!

When I got to the race, the place was rocking. I have to say that the Rev3 group puts on a nice triathlon. They market well and have good signage and plenty of booths for shopping.

Being that I now had three and a half hours to kill, I just walked around. I probably looked like a stalker because I was there for so long. I sat and watched some of the Olympic racers finish and tried to draw some inspiration from them. I did.

After a little while, I went down to the swim start. This time, I was committed to swimming in the wetsuit before the race. Heather Golnick was down there giving some instruction to people who wanted some swimming tips.

I was one of the first people down there and, thus, one of the first few people to put his wetsuit on. Because of the way that my wetsuit zips, I asked a woman next to me to help zip me up. She did.

When she zipped me up, she must have been off by a couple of teeth in the zipper because as soon as I bent over, *zip!* It came unzipped, but not the good way, the bad way.

I now had a zipper that was stuck in the up position, while the rest of it actually hung open. If you have ever had this happen to one of your zippers you know that it is virtually impossible to unzip the zipper without destroying it. Imagine doing it on a $600 wetsuit.

For some reason, I wasn't actually mad about it. The woman didn't do anything wrong, and my initial thought was that maybe it would be better for me. After all, both times I tried to drown;

I thought about just unzipping the suit but was afraid I might get water in it.

So I jumped in. Stroke, stroke, stroke, breathe. Stroke, stroke, stroke, breathe. I was doing it.

Not surprisingly, swimming with the wetsuit unzipped actually worked for me. I am sure I was not the most aerodynamic guy in the water, and I probably looked like an idiot, but it worked for me. I was thrilled.

I got out of the water somewhat like I did at Todd Wiley's class and gave myself a mini fist pump. Big dork!

I managed to kill the rest of the day and get into my hotel. I had stopped at the local supermarket and bought some wheat bagels and fruit for breakfast, along with a giant container of water.

If someone would have been able to see what went on in that hotel room the rest of the night, they would have thought I was a meth dealer mixing up batches of product. I spent a large portion of the night trying to mix my nutrition in my water bottles without any actual kitchen utensils. I had water bottles and flasks for my FuelBelt all over the room. You would have thought that I would have learned something about water displacement at some point in my life, but I missed that lesson. I was trying to jam stuff into places, and powder and water were flying all over the room. It was really quite a spectacle.

The rest of the evening went fine. I ate a light dinner and was in bed before ten.

I made it to transition early as usual. In the grand scheme of things, this wasn't an overly large race. I put all my stuff where it needed to be and then just hung out.

One of the coolest things about the Rev3 races is the amount of pros that they have. Even though they have their own area in transition, they are still in the same transition that I am. That's the coolest thing about this sport. Imagine playing tennis and having Roger Federer next to you. It would never happen. In triathlon, you are in the same race as all those people you see in the magazines.

I just sat there and watched them prepare. They all have zero percent body fat, and I am pretty sure I could throw all of them from one side of transition to the other without much effort.

One minute you were standing next to Craig Alexander, the next it was Desiree Ficker, then DeDe Griesbauer, and then Matty Reed. It was pretty cool. At some point close to the start of the race, I turned around to see Natascha Badmann entering transition. She had won six Ironman world championships.

Once race time came, we all made our way down to the water, amateurs and pros alike. Over time, it seems that they have smartened up and now give the pros a ten-minute head start. I suppose that's so no hotshot amateurs get in the water and foul up their chances of winning.

Being near the water and seeing all of those pros go off was cool. They looked just as nervous as I was, although I'm sure they weren't. They also run at a full sprint into the water, while most of us "normal" people just march out at a slow cadence.

After a few waves and countless butterflies, my wave was called into the water. Bang, we were off.

As planned the day before, I got into the water with my wet-suit unzipped. I started to swim and quickly found a rhythm. While I didn't feel any better or worse than any other day, I could swim today.

Overall, the swim went well. I only had to stop three or four times to clean my goggles, but everything else went fine. I wasn't overly tired and seemed to keep up with most of the other folks around me. I got out of the water, having successfully completed the swim. I didn't drown; I didn't doggy paddle. It was my first successful freestyle swim with a wetsuit on, even if it wasn't zipped.

Getting my bike and moving out of transition was somewhat exciting for me. Most of the races I had done to date had disastrous swims, so when I got to transition, most of the bikes were already gone. Not this time. I was right in the middle of everyone.

I started out on the bike like I was someone important. I felt good and still had a lot of energy. This made me feel like I could fly, which I did. I was whizzing by people and enjoying every minute of it. My bike was fast, as was I.

That lasted about one mile. When we hit the first hill of the course, just about everybody that I had passed, passed me. How humiliating. You look like a giant jackass when you whiz by people on the flats but have them pass you two minutes later.

The first hill crushed me. I had heard that this course was hilly, but I wasn't expecting it to be this bad. Believe it or not, where I live outside of Philadelphia is very hilly. I thought I had put in a lot of hill time. Not even close.

When I got off the first hill, we hit another, then another, then another. I honestly felt like the entire race was uphill. These were not hills; they were climbs. Big climbs. They were not even a little bit easy. Even the tiny people who were in great shape had some level of difficulty.

It was maybe around mile twelve where I first started telling myself that I couldn't do this. I was literally saying, "I can't do this. I can't do this," as I rode up each hill.

Every time we got a break and got a downhill, we were headed right back up before we knew it. This race was kicking my butt. I had used every ounce of guts, stamina, and energy that I could to get up those hills. I even had to get off my bike and walk up one, pretending that I had a cramp.

I spent the better part of three hours in complete misery. It was literally the hardest physical thing I have ever done—big, steep, long hills, one after the other, followed by my incessant brain telling me that "I can't do this." That's the alcoholic in me. Always negative.

My wrists hurt, my back hurt, my neck hurt, and my rear end hurt. I honestly don't know how I kept going. I was counting every foot I moved forward and sometimes cursing out loud. I had again made a decision in the last two miles that I was never doing a triathlon again, let alone an Ironman.

I had spent at least half of the bike ride not only filling my head with negative thoughts but deciding how I couldn't possibly do the Ironman. If I couldn't do something that was only half the distance, how could I ever do a full Ironman?

Or course, this awful bike ride ended on a tough uphill that made me watch all of the people who were already off their bikes run past me as they ran downhill. Argh!

They were yelling, "Come on, you can do it," while I was cursing at every one of them inside.

When I got to transition, I was so happy to be off the bike that I didn't care that I had to run a half-marathon. Had I seen a six-foot-three ten-year-old, I probably would have walked over to him and given him my bike.

I started off the run pretty well. Given the fact that I had absolutely trashed my legs during the bike, I was happy that I could run at all. It was hot but not unbearably so.

I struggled through the first mile of the run to the first water station. It felt so good to stop, but I managed to get myself running again. During mile number two, I could tell that my legs were hurting. All of those big, long hills had really done a number on me.

I made it to the second aid station at mile two but barely. I started to run out of the aid station but probably only made it a hundred yards. From there, I started to walk/run every hundred yards. Walk a hundred, run a hundred.

After a couple minutes of that, I saw a big guy like me a few hundred yards in front of me. He was doing the same thing that I was doing, but he seemed to be struggling a bit more than I was. I can say that, but at the time, he was still in front of me.

I eventually caught up to him, and we started walking together. His name was Frank. Frank and I were to be best friends for the next eleven miles.

When Frank and I started talking, we were wallowing in the same misery. He was about the same size as me and was really struggling with the run. We never officially made a decision but just sort of decided to stick together.

At first, I was pushing him to try to run. While I wasn't in any way flying, I could run a little bit. My nutrition plan had really paid off. In addition to that, I was doing Ironman Lake Placid at the end of July. He was doing Ironman Louisville at the end of August. That meant that I had a full month more training than he did. I also don't think that he had his nutrition down quite yet.

After the initial meeting, I pushed him to run to the bottom of the next hill. I want to be clear that I was not a gazelle floating effortlessly through the air. I was trudging. We both made it.

When we got to the bottom of the hill, Frank said, "Go ahead. I can't run anymore. I'm cramping up."

I said, "Dude, I'm not setting any records, I'll stay with you, and we'll get each other through it."

Frank and I became instant friends. I would imagine that it would be like being in a marine platoon or being on a football team. You have an instant brotherhood by going through things with people.

Frank and I proceeded to walk and talk the rest of the race. We laughed and had fun. We messed around with the people at the aid stations and talked about *Curb Your Enthusiasm* in between. I'm not sure he knows it, but he really helped me.

The reason I had known that my nutrition plan had worked fairly well was that I actually felt okay. My legs were trashed from the bike, but I actually didn't feel that terrible. I wasn't cramping, and I could actually walk at a decent clip.

I don't know exactly what mile it was, but at some point, we started doing the math on how long it would take us to complete the half-marathon. We figured at the pace we were walking and where we already were, it would take us about three hours.

I was ecstatic. This was a real turning point for me and the first point where I truly believed that I could do the Ironman. Doing that half-Ironman with Frank made me realize that if I had to, I could walk a full Ironman marathon in about six hours. I have always been a fast walker. Even before I grew. Once I became 6'3", I could really fly. My family and friends have always complained about me. I walk too fast, and they yell at me to slow down.

I had spent the better part of fifty-six miles telling myself that I couldn't do this and that it was too hard. During the run, I had completely flipped the other way.

One of the concerns that you have when doing an Ironman is the time limit. That had been my concern from day one. I knew I could do the distance; it was more a question of how long it would take me.

To finish an Ironman, you have seventeen hours, not one second more. If you finish at 17:00:01, you get a DNF (did not finish). I thought I could do the swim in about 1.5 hours but was not sure about the bike. Lake Placid was also very hilly, and I still had some doubts. Either way, if I could finish the bike in 7.5 hours, that would give me eight hours to do the marathon. If I walked the whole thing, I could finish in fifteen.

I had gone from complete dread to overwhelming joy in one morning in one race.

Frank and I spent over three hours together talking about family, careers, training, and anything else we could think of. I smiled and enjoyed every minute of it. We laughed like two old school chums reliving the good times. The truth was that we were just getting each other through the race.

When we came around the final few hills, we passed a bunch of people who had finished the race going to their cars, all of them commenting on how hard the course was. This made us both feel a bit better. Even the hardcore people were a bit shell-shocked, it seemed.

Frank and I split up for only about thirty seconds so we could both run across the finish line on our own. I ran the last quarter of a mile, followed shortly by Frank. We hugged and high fived each other and looked around at the now ghost town finish line. It didn't matter; we finished.

Frank and I walked up to transition together and got each other's e-mail addresses. We still keep in touch today and are thinking about doing another Ironman next year together.

Another race. Another set of lessons learned. It's amazing what I can do sober.

THE FINAL STRETCH

Sitting down after the half-Ironman was done and looking at what had transpired gave me a chance to recognize one of my biggest problems. Just as it is important to sit down and look at the outcomes in your life and see what lessons can be learned, I tried to do the same thing after my races. What did I do good? What did I do bad?

One of the things that I recognized almost immediately was how negative I was. I spent a large part of that racing saying, "I can't do this, this is too hard, these people are better than me, they are smaller."

I also realized that with each race I had done, I had learned something. While somebody else may have been smarter than me and learned everything in their first race, I needed each challenge to teach me something. In sobriety, we often say, "Pain is the touchstone of spiritual progress." I really do believe that. Sometimes you have to go through what you have to go through to learn and appreciate where you are now.

Having recognized the huge hole I had in my mental game, I did what I did with everything else; I logged onto the Internet and looked for a solution on Amazon.com.

I immediately started searching for books on mental training. I searched for a few hours and came up with two books that I thought could help me, *Mental Training* by Jim Taylor and Teri Schneider and *The Warrior Elite* by Dick Couch.

Mental Training was a book about exactly that. It talked about the body's natural defense system against pain and how it tries to stop us. It also gave many different strategies from positive reinforcement and thinking to visualization.

The Warrior Elite was a book about Navy SEALS. You would have to have grown up on a different planet to not know how tough and hardcore these guys were. I had seen enough shows on TV to know that these people where the toughest people on the planet. They did things that were physically and mentally impossible. I wanted to know how they did it.

Dick's book essentially followed a class of recruits from day one of SEAL school through graduation. It showed every part of what they had to do and how. With every page I turned, I became more and more convinced that 99 percent of what they were doing was mental. Yes, there were strong, tough guys, but the ones who made it were the ones who were the strongest mentally.

I read that book cover-to-cover in a week, and I wanted more. It inspired me more than anything else I had ever read. It showed me that if I believed I could do it, I could. I didn't have to shoot anyone or get out of the ocean and roll around in sand. I just had to tune my mind.

Between those two books, I thought I now had an idea of what I needed to do mentally. While I was not there yet, I had a vision and some inspiration. I don't know why, but I think the only thing in the world I would like to be more than an Ironman is a Navy SEAL.

The second thing that I realized after that half-Ironman was that I didn't know how to ride a bike. As stupid as that may sound, it's true.

Despite the fact that the race had a ridiculous amount of tough hills, I should have done better. In hindsight, I realize that part of my problem was me. I climb hills on a bike much like I would climb a ladder; I use power. I use all the energy and power in my legs to propel me up the hill. What this does to me is it turns my legs to Jell-O.

I don't know when or why, but I realized after that race that's it not the power that gets you up the hill; it's the spinning of your legs that does it.

I had heard the term *cadence* a million times. But I had grown up on a bike. I arrogantly thought I didn't need any instruction on how to ride a bike. *Anyone can ride a bike,* I thought. I was wrong about that.

You can climb a hill much easier if you use an easy gear and just keep your legs moving versus trying to use brute force to get you to the top. In all of the races I had done thus far, I used brute strength. By the time I would get to the run, I was out of gas. No diet supplement out there could bring me back from that.

If I had to give you an example of what it was like, imagine going to the gym and doing squats with heavy weights for an hour straight and then running ten miles. That's what it was like. When I finally figured out how to do it, it changed everything for me.

I do want to say that one of the things that I could have done that would have made my life and my training much easier was to get a coach. There is no shortage of coaches out there that can help you. They can design specific plans for you and help you every step of the way. I'm not really sure why I didn't get one; I just didn't. That meant that every single thing that I learned, I had to learn on my own. While I was smart enough to ask questions, I had to be smart enough to ask the right question to get the right answer. Had I gotten a coach early on, I may have saved myself a lot of heartache.

Despite the lessons I had learned and my renewed confidence that I could finish, I still suffered from a lack of motivation.

Training for the Ironman was the longest amount of consecutive training I had ever done. Even if you were a diehard athlete in high school, your season was not usually eleven months long.

Here I was, an alcoholic who had no real history of long training, going at it for almost a year. No matter how hard I tried or how much I tried to convince myself to keep pushing, those last weeks of training were torture. Staring at a black line at the bottom of a pool for 1.5 hours three times a week was a killer. Knowing that I had to ride my bike for five hours on Saturday was a killer.

I just kept telling myself to put one foot in front of the other, but I was starting to hate it.

The funny thing about it was that the training wasn't really that bad; it was the thought of the training that killed me. Knowing that I had to do the training was what got me. But when I was actually doing it, I didn't really mind.

A lot of people asked me during my training, "How do you do it?" I gave everyone the same answer. "It's not the physical part that gets you; it's the mental part." Unlike my poor mental state in most of my races, I was strong enough mentally to follow through with the training plan. As silly as it sounds, that's really the hardest part. Getting in a pool when there is three feet of snow outside takes a lot of mental focus. Making yourself run when it is pouring rain outside takes a lot of focus. Fitting it all into an already busy schedule requires a lot of determination. If you haven't done it, it's hard to explain.

The only other exciting things that happened before the race were a quick little trip down to Disney World with the kids at the end of June, and I turned forty in July. And, oh yeah, I got hit by a car.

Having learned my lesson about being able to miss a workout now and then really helped me in Disney. I didn't freak out if I missed something and actually learned to enjoy myself. I was smart enough to realize that being on my feet walking around for twelve hours a day didn't need to be topped off with a two-hour run every night.

It was hot, but we had fun.

My fortieth birthday was just that. While some people make a big deal about milestones like that, it was just another birthday to me. I'm not one of those people who freaks out about getting older. In fact, I have my own theory. "Enjoy forty when you are forty because when you are fifty, you would pay to be forty." Enjoy the age you are when you have it, not when you wish you have it. It may sound stupid, but that's the way I look at it.

Around the weekend of the Fourth of July, my wife's family rented a house in Ocean City, New Jersey, for the week. Because I had already taken a week of vacation for Disney and more vacation for the Ironman, I had only gone down for the weekend.

My stepmother and I share the same birthday. That weekend, I was starting my taper for the Ironman so I only needed to ride my bike for four hours. It's funny, but four hours was actually a light day for me at that point.

It's roughly thirty miles from Ocean City, New Jersey, to Cape May, New Jersey, so I had decided to ride my bike to my dad's house that Saturday morning to say happy birthday. Two birds with one stone! Round trip, it should take me just about four hours.

The ride over was uneventful. It's a flat ride, but if anyone ever tells you it's easy, they're lying. It's the wind that gets you. When you get far enough away from the ocean for the wind to stop blowing, the bay breeze gets you. Oftentimes, you get it from both sides.

I had made it about halfway back without incident. In fact, I made it to Avalon, New Jersey, which is a great place for a bike ride. It's a fairly rich town, so you don't really have to worry about too many drunken young kids, and the roads have designated bike lanes.

I was moving along at a fairly good pace, passing all of the leisure riders and people with dogs. I was coming up to a street when I noticed a purple PT Cruiser coming from the opposite direction that I was traveling. He needed to make a left-hand turn, which meant he had to turn in front of me. I slowed down a bit but never touched the breaks. He inched out a bit at a time, which made me think that he was looking. I had to be going at least 20 mph. I was watching him the whole time.

When I finally got to the actual intersection, he hit the gas and tried to make his left. I was going so fast that I had no choice but to hit him.

I locked up both breaks, which made both my tires start to skid immediately. I skidded about five feet before the bike went sideways and I went over the handlebars. I stopped short of actually hitting his car. Had I actually hit his car, they would have taken me away in an ambulance.

I don't even think that I had completely gotten up before I was cursing at this guy. He was a younger guy who just wasn't paying attention. He looked like he had just seen a ghost. He was as white as you could get. He was clearly shaken up and scared to death. It didn't help that I was screaming at him at the top of my lugs for the whole city to hear.

Another rider from the other side of the road saw the whole thing and came over and tried to help me. He helped me pick up all my water bottles and all of the other stuff that was now all over the road. I was still yelling at this guy as he parked his car. Yelling may be a bit of an understatement.

Remarkably, I didn't get hurt at all. I had a few very minor scuffs but nothing of any significance. I must have fallen the right way. If I reacted even a half a second later, it would have been a much different story.

When he finally came up to me, he apologized a hundred times, still scared to death. I told him that I didn't have any interest in a long, drawn out insurance case but that if my bike was broken, he was fixing it.

I sat there with the Good Samaritan, and we checked over my bike. The frame wasn't cracked, and the rims were still straight. Amazing. Not only did I come out okay; most of my bike did, too. The only thing wrong was that I had a cracked break lever and the gears where out of whack.

I showed the guy the break lever, got his insurance information, and we parted ways.

I don't know how I came out of that crash with only a few bruises, but I did. I hadn't even hit the ground during the crash, and I was already thinking about missing Lake Placid. If it were a movie, they would have shown me in slow motion flying through the air with pictures of Lake Placid flying by.

In the end, I got my bike fixed and tuned up. I sent him a picture of the broken lever, along with a link to Amazon to show him how much it cost. I apologized for cursing at him and calling him every name I could think of. I also told him that I didn't really feel like going through his insurance company. I asked him for a check for $190. He sent me one for $200. We were both thrilled to be dealing with another nice, rational human being.

While my wife was not all that thrilled with the giant red marks on my back, it could have been worse. I could have hit the car or broken something or missed the race. It was a crappy morning for me, but the way I looked at it was that I was still on the right side of the dirt.

"THE WAITING IS THE HARDEST PART"

I'm not sure if Tom Petty officially coined that phrase or not, but man is it true. The week prior to my Ironman followed the same hectic pattern I had been in for the past six months. Tuesday began with my alarm clock going off at 4:30 a.m. so that I could get ready for my 6:30 a.m. flight to the tropical paradise known as Memphis, Tennessee. The trip was fine, with the exception of the heat. I did what I needed to do for work and caught a flight that got me into Philadelphia at midnight on Wednesday. Yes, midnight. As you may guess I was a bit exhausted come Thursday morning. Nevertheless, we packed the car and were off to Lake Placid by 9:30 a.m.

The drive up was uneventful. It took us about 7.5 hours and four bathroom stops to get there, but we got there. (Thank God for iTouches and GameBoys.)

If you haven't been to Lake Placid, I highly recommend it, at least if you appreciate nature and beautiful scenery. If you can't make it a whole weekend without a Bed, Bath, and Beyond trip, then it's probably not for you.

While some people may argue, upstate New York is not all that different from upstate Pennsylvania. Lots and lots of trees, streams and friendly folks all around. I can't help but wonder how many people wish they could find a way to make a living in these places so they could live there all the time. I know I did.

The first thing that crossed my mind when we pulled into town was, "How in the world did they have the Olympics here?" I'm serious; it's not near anything. If you threw a dart at the map and it landed in the middle of Kansas, it wouldn't be any more remote than Lake Placid. The mountains are gorgeous, and you can tell the ski slopes are wicked, but it is in the middle of nowhere.

We got to our hotel right around dinnertime. It was a quaint, little place called the Adirondack Motel. The nice thing about this place was that it was set right on Saranac Lake. Because there are 3,100 people that sign up for the Ironman, we couldn't get a place that was near downtown Lake Placid. All the better; we ended up having a great time at this place.

It didn't take long before the nerves started hitting me. After we had arrived and eaten dinner, we made our way to downtown Lake Placid. It's a quaint, little town right out of a movie. For all its beauty, I couldn't help but think that it was probably twice as gorgeous in the winter. It is basically a one-lane street lined with shops, shops, and more shops. I imagine it is what Vail probably looks like.

We weren't there for very long when we made our way down to the Olympic Oval. The Olympic Oval is an outdoor speed-skating oval that is right outside the Olympic Center. For those of you like me that have never seen a speed-skating oval, it's about the size of a high school running track, right down to the grass in the center. In fact, it didn't hit me for a while that it wasn't actually a running track.

When you come down to the end of Main Street in Lake Placid, you can stand at the top and look down on the oval.

It was about two seconds after I saw all of the Ford Ironman tents and bike racks and signs that I had my first (of many to come) nervous breakdown. Holy crap! I'm doing an Ironman. I'm sure there is some bizarre psychological reason behind it, but simply seeing the whole thing hit home. I was really here. I was really going to do this. What if I couldn't do it? What if this was a waste? The money, the time, the sacrifice. What if I couldn't pull this off? I'm just a drunk. Who the hell do I think I am? All of my negative alcoholic thoughts came pouring out.

One of the things that I have thus far failed to convey is the amount of people that my wife told about this little adventure. She told *everyone!* If I went to her work, people asked me about it. If I was coaching my daughter's softball game, people asked me about it. If I went to a family party, people asked me about it. Realistically, I was partly miffed at her for doing that. I know that I had learned that if you sign up for something and tell people, you are more likely to finish the race. But this was becoming a lot of pressure. People at my work had found out. People at the gym had found out. It was becoming breaking news everywhere I went.

Now, being an alcoholic, I isolate by default. It's what I do. Here I was now, with a hundred people looking through a magnifying glass at me. At least, that's what it felt like.

That's the kind of pressure that I was putting on myself. I knew at the time, and even more now, that I was the only one putting pressure on myself, but for some reason, it doesn't make it go away. Like I always say to my father, "Intellectually, I get it; emotionally, I have no idea."

The rest of that night was fairly uneventful, with the exception of the desperate text I sent to my sober friend John at midnight, which said, "In Lake Placid, half-scared out of my mind."

He simply replied with his thirty-two years of sobriety and said, "Good, the nervous energy will help you. I'll say a prayer for you."

The next morning, we woke up and got ourselves together. The only downside to the place we were staying was that it was small. If we were in a fraternity house, they would have probably squeezed another two bodies in there. As it was, we weren't a frat, and with four people, it was tight, especially since I had my bike and all of my gear in the room as well. It was one of those situations where every time you moved, you had to move something else to the open space where you just were so you could get around.

After the hour-long ritual that the kids took to get out of bed, we all got dressed and headed to town. One of the irritating things that you have to do at a race of this size is check in ahead of time. In all honesty, it's not just the Ironman; I had to do it for the half-marathon and half-Ironman as well. However, at the Ironman, you have to check in two days before the race. I'm sure it's some deal they have with the town so that they can get as much business as possible. But when you have a couple of kids who are looking for stuff to do, Ironman registration is not at the top of their list.

We pulled into town a little after ten. After spending ten minutes looking for a parking spot, we finally made our way to the high school on the other side of the speed skating oval. Holy smokes! The line was already a hundred yards long.

Panic attack number two!

It had hit me the night before when we were walking around town, but I thought maybe it was just a sampling of people and not all of them. But I was wrong; it was more than a sampling. All these people were in shape! I know that may sound like a bit of an absurd statement coming from someone standing in line at an Ironman, but these people were really in shape. The one thing that I realized early in my quest was that by and large, I was bigger than most of these people. When I met Craig Alexander at the Rev 3 Half-Ironman, he came up to my chin. If he weighs more than 140 pounds, I'd be shocked. Mirinda Carfrae, who came in second in the women's division last year at the World Championships, is about 5'4" and 115 with five-pound shoes on. I am not close to either of those people in size. While I was standing in line, I saw a bunch of people that looked much more like them and a lot less like me—small, zero body fat, and no kids with them.

There I was with my kids, the wife, and twenty-five pounds of extra body that most of them didn't have. If I was anorexic, I would have still weighed more than most of them. The best way I could describe it was that there were about fifty professionals there that were trying to win the race. Then there were a whole slew of people there that were the tree bark and granola eating, zero body fat, die hard exercisers. You know who they are. They are the ones at the gym that have a matching outfit for each day of the week. Usually, they are too small or too tight, especially the guys. They know everyone and are constantly looking in the mirror or checking their heart rate monitor. Then there are the people like me, people who were changing their life or want to prove something to themselves. These are the true Ironmen to me. If you weigh 120 pounds and routinely run a three-hour marathon, then the Ironman isn't as big of a deal to you. If you used to weigh 260 pounds and this is your first marathon, then you are really doing something special.

While there is absolutely no such thing as an easy Ironman, I do think that there was definitely a line between those people who lived this life all the time and the people like me who had to make it work with all of their other duties.

Either way, I felt out of place. Here I was among all of these people with killer physiques, and I still, despite twenty-plus hours of training per week, couldn't see my abs.

When we finally managed to get into the gymnasium at the school, sufficiently soaked from the rain, I got back in line and started signing my life away. As with anything that has risk in it nowadays, you have to sign all of the waivers they can come up with before you race. I think people that have surgery have to sign fewer things than I did prior to this race.

After signing my life away, they had me step on the scale. If I wasn't already self-conscious enough, here I was now getting on a scale in front of people. I want to add that I couldn't care less about my weight in terms of vanity. I care more because I felt like a slow giant compared to most of these people. When I got on the scale, I looked down, and it read 205. I looked at the girl who was filing out my paperwork and said, "Do I win a prize for the highest number today?"

She just smiled and said, "No, there have been a few that have you beat." I laughed and smiled all the way through the rest of registration. If I was going to do this, I told myself that I was going to smile as much as I could. I thanked every volunteer I could and made my way out into the rain with the family.

After registration, we walked around Lake Placid for a bit and then decided to hit the nature center about fifteen miles away. It was a cool, museum-type place that had everything from live fish to a stuffed moose. It gave a great history of the Adirondack Mountains and the indigenous wildlife that lived there. It turned out to be a great place to spend a rainy afternoon.

The only downside to the nature center was the size. We were in and out of there in less than two hours, including lunch, which when you are trying to kill a rainy afternoon with two kids is not the best scenario.

After the nature center, we made our way back to the hotel, which my wife and I were both secretly dreading. What were we going to do with two girls in a small hotel room at two o'clock in the afternoon while it's raining?

Remarkably, fishing was the answer! The rain had let up enough that it wasn't really an issue. So we made our way down to the private dock that the hotel had on one of the local lakes. We all took turns going in the canoes and kayaks until they finally talked me into fishing. Earlier that morning, my younger daughter and I had gone and bought a fishing license and some worms. I brought all of my fishing gear from home with me. We had two rods and two kids. Perfect.

I had taken the older one, Gabriella, trout fishing earlier this year, and she liked it. She caught a few fish and was surprisingly patient. We fished for a few hours, and she never complained. That's the first rule in spending time fishing with your father; if you want to get invited back, don't complain.

This, however, was Emily's first fishing excursion. We went over to the dock, and I put a worm on the hook for her. I showed her how to lower it into the water and *wham*! She had a fish within fifteen seconds. For those of you would-be parents at home, this is what I call a small miracle. Letting an eight-year-old girl catch a fish on her first try in less than a minute is just about the only thing that will keep her fishing. And it did. She caught one fish after another. They both did. They were all small sunnies, but it kept them busy and interested. Even my wife took a few turns. She hadn't been fishing since we first started dating. In fact, she caught the biggest fish of all of us. She pulled in a nice smallmouth bass. There were even a few instances when I left the dock that they tried to get the fish off the hook themselves. By *they*, I mean my wife.

Of course, taking girls fishing does have one downside. None of them want to touch a worm. They will touch the side of a fish if you hold it. They may even put fake bait on the hook. But not one of them wanted to touch a worm, which meant that no matter where I was, when they lost their worm, I had to run over and put a new one on. I will give my wife credit and say that she tried, but you would have thought I had asked her to eat one.

The day ended up being one of the nicest days we had together as a family in a long time. I don't think I thought about the Ironman once while we were fishing. For two parents that were worried that the kids would be bored to death in the Adirondacks, it was a nice reminder that you don't always need the electronics and television. Sometimes you just need each other. Sometimes!

The next day was bike drop-off day. Usually in a race like this, you have to drop off your bike and additional clothes bags the day before the race. I'm not really sure why. Probably because they don't want 3,100 people all showing up at 5:00 a.m. on race day at the same time. Unlike registration day, we couldn't even find a parking spot. My wife drove me as close to the entrance as she could, and I hopped out with my gear. It took me all of about five minutes to put my bike on the rack and find my clothing rack.

The clothing rack is nothing but a metal rack with hooks on it that you hang your run and bike gear on. Because you are going for 140.6 miles, you end up having a lot of supplies. In the bike bag, you have your helmet, sunglasses, sunscreen, and anything else you may need on the bike. In the run bag, you have your sneakers, a change of socks, more suntan lotion, maybe a hat or a visor, and a fuel belt with some other kind of fuel that you will carry during the run. After each part of the race, you always end up back near the transition area. So when you are done with the swim you take off your wetsuit and grab your bike bag and go into the changing tent. You put on all your bike stuff and jam your wetsuit back into that bag. Then you go get your bike. Same thing happens on the run. Then volunteers take your bag and put them back on the rack for you. I thanked any volunteer that got within eyesight of me. Without them, a race like this would be impossible.

I spent all of about five minutes in transition setting up my bike and bags. Honestly, I can't figure out what some of the people where doing there. They were checking their bike and rechecking and rechecking. I just remember feeling like I should be doing something. But I didn't. I had my bike tuned up and fixed after my crash; my tires were good, and I packed my bags myself. Despite feeling like I should be doing something, I trusted what I did and left, leaving all the "granolas" behind me.

While I considered the previous day's fishing fun to be the best part of the family side of the vacation, I would probably be overruled by the three girls who quickly found out how much they liked horseback riding. We already knew that Gabriella loved horses. She had been to camp before and had liked any book or movie that had to do with horses since she was little. Emily was the one we were a bit worried about. Emily is a very friendly, loving little kid. But if something has a pulse, she's afraid of it, literally, dogs, cats, hamsters, anything. If it is breathing and can lick or touch her, she is scared to death of it. She's been like that since she was born. We have no idea why.

Now here we were taking her horseback riding. Up until about five minutes before we started, we were under the impression that she was going to be on the horse by herself, something I seemed to be the only one worrying about. She was doing all that she could not to cry, but you could tell she was getting nervous, especially when she actually saw the horses. Lucky for us, the guide ended up asking us if we wanted one of the ranch hands to walk around with her, which we gratefully accepted. She ended up having a ball, as did the rest of us.

One of the things my wife had asked me before we went was whether or not I could go because of my butt. Meaning, wasn't the horse going to give me a sore butt before the race? I had decided that I had spent enough time on that little bike seat that I could probably ride that thing to New Jersey naked and it wouldn't bother me. Lucky for me, I was right.

The final thing we had done that day was the cause of my third and final nervous breakdown. My alcoholism once again reared its ugly head.

When we got back from horseback riding, we spent the day at the lake again, fishing, swimming, and canoeing. The unspoken idea was that we would get dinner somewhere locally so I could be in bed at a decent hour. Apparently, having this as an "unspoken" rule was not my best idea.

It turned out that when we went to the local town, which was less than a few football fields away, the buildings were just for show. Every last one of them was closed. So we ended up driving into downtown Lake Placid. Going to Lake Placid itself was not a problem. Getting a table at 8:00 p.m. for dinner was the problem. When we finally got seated, dinner seemed to take forever. I'm not sure if it actually took forever or if it just seemed like it did because I didn't see a single other person who was doing the race in town at that time.

The reason that I knew this was because when you register for the race they put a blue Ironman band on your wrist. You can't get in and out of transition without one, and you have to wear it for all four days. So it's easy to tell the people who are doing the race from the volunteers and tourists.

I, it seemed, was the only person in the race who was actually out in Lake Placid at 9:00 p.m., then 9:30 p.m., then 10:00 p.m. I was slowly starting to melt down in my own mind.

It's a weird feeling being in a town that has been packed with people for the past three nights that is now virtually empty, except for my family.

It took a full dinner and a stuffed animal store or two, but I finally lost it and yelled at the family that we needed to leave. Why saying something to them during dinner in a civilized way was not my first option I don't know. Either way, I lost it, and we ended up leaving.

Part of the reason I was mad was that I still needed to stop at the supermarket to buy a few things. I needed water, ice, and something for breakfast for the next day.

I stopped at the supermarket and got everything that I needed. Of course, it took me forever to get out of there because of all of the obnoxious people on their cell phones standing in line in front of me. If I could have thrown one of them through the window and still made the race, I would have.

When we got home, I was still mad. I mixed all the water bottles and put them on ice. I got all of my nutrition together for the next day and finally got in bed with my jaw clenched.

I finally got to bed around eleven thirty, the night before the longest race of my life.

Race Day

I had tossed and turned most of the night. I suppose I should have known that I wouldn't sleep that well. It turned out that it didn't really matter what time I went to bed. I later found out this is fairly normal, especially during your first Ironman.

My wife and I had set the alarm for 5:00 a.m. The idea was for her to drop me off at the race and come back later. She kept asking me over and over again what they should do during the day. I had insisted that they go do something fun and not wait around all day. Odds were they weren't going to see me, and getting two kids to sit still all day was pretty much impossible.

I told my wife to come back around 9:00 p.m. I thought if I had a great day, I would be done around 8:00 p.m., and if I had a terrible day, I would be done at midnight. Three hours was the longest they would have to wait, unless they took me off on a stretcher. And in that case, I would probably be done early.

When we drove into Lake Placid, it was mobbed. You would have thought that the Beatles had reunited. There were cars and people everywhere, especially down by transition. We sat in traffic for about five minutes when I decided to get out and walk the rest of the way. It was only a couple hundred yards and that way my wife didn't have to wait two hours to get out.

She pulled over to the side and wished me luck. I thanked her and gave her a kiss.

I walked down to transition through the circus environment. It was rocking! This was the most people I had seen upright and not hung over at 5:30 a.m. in my life.

I made my way into transition with the thirty pounds of water bottles that I had mixed the night before. I literally had eight water bottles for the bike, one to drink pre-race, an extra for my run bag, and four flasks of nutrition for the run.

I quickly put four bottles on my bike and then headed for the special needs section. Special needs is just that. Because of the length of the race and the sheer amount of fuel that you need to consume, you can't carry it all with you. So there is a special needs section at the halfway point of both the bike and the run. You can put whatever you want in there, PowerBars, gels, pretzels, cookies, extra water bottles, you name it.

I simply put four water bottles in my bike bag for the second half of the bike and a spare water bottle and flasks for the run. Once I finished up at special needs, I made my way back down to transition and got marked up. Then the waiting began.

I actually got to transition at a much better time than I had in most of my previous events. Part of it was because I brought my bike and clothes the day before. I like to think that I am actually getting smarter in my old age. So I ended up only having to kill about an hour before the race.

The other thing that was nice about this race was that it had a mass swim start (more about that later), which meant that we were all starting at 7:00 a.m. and I didn't have to wait until 8:30 for my wave.

I wandered around transition for a while, checking out all of the other carbon-fiber rocket ships. Most of them had wheels that cost more than my first two cars.

At 6:30 they closed transition and kicked everyone out. That meant that all of us started walking toward the water. At the Lake Placid Ironman, the actual lake is about a quarter mile away from transition. So there we were, 3,100 of us in bare feet, with goggles in one hand and our wetsuits and swim caps in the other, walking toward the lake.

We stood around, waiting to get into the water like lambs waiting for the slaughter. I happened to be standing next to Ryan and Trista from *The Bachelor*. The only reason I even knew who they were was because he did the Ironman in Kona and they talked about it when it aired on TV.

You would have thought those two invented plutonium. People were coming up to them asking for autographs and getting their pictures taken non-stop. In all honesty, they were very gracious. They probably should have told half those people to pound sand, but they didn't. They posed for one photo after another.

After I got tired of watching the Ryan and Trista show, I made my way down to the sand. There were 3,100 people all trying to stay out of the water, while race organizers were trying to get them all in. We were all trying to conserve our energy; they were trying to fit everybody in.

With about ten minutes to go, I finally got in the water. I had done a practice swim the day before when the girls were fishing and made a decision to swim with my wetsuit zipped all the way up. I know, another unproven, untested race day decision. In case I haven't mentioned it before, just about everyone in the free world will tell you, "If you didn't practice it, don't do it on race day." My theory was that if I started swimming and had trouble, I would simply unzip it. I wasn't sure how, but that was my thought.

The Lake Placid swim start is essentially a huge circle. The starting line is on one side; land is on the other three sides. Lake Placid also has a mass swim start. If the mass swim start sounds scary, then I'm not doing it justice; it's insane. I have heard it described as like being in a blender or being in a washing machine. Neither is far off. Because this is the case, you end up with two distinct groups of people, those who are going to start swimming when the cannon goes off and those of us who all think we will wait five minutes for the commotion to die down.

It certainly sounds like a good idea to wait, until you look around and 1,500 other people have the same idea. This puts 1,500 at the starting line treading water and another 1,500 on land waiting to get in five minutes later.

About a minute or so before the race, I looked out and essentially saw a great, big, open space of water in front of me. So I made an on-the-spot executive decision that I might as well just go for it. There were people everywhere; if I went into a mass start expecting not to get touched, I would have been nuts. So I said a prayer, jumped in the water, and waited for the bang. Then it came.

Bang!

A cannon had signaled the start of a day I had been waiting on for almost a year. All of the blood, sweat, and tears that I had put into this would come down to this one day, in this one place. *Could I do it? Would I be able to do it?* Can some regular drunk of a guy like me actually do this? We would soon find out.

As with anything in life, the worry about something tends to be worse than when it actually happens. I had worked myself into a frenzy the past few days thinking about the swim. *What if I had another meltdown? What if I tried to drown?* You name it, I thought it. But this time, when the gun went off, I just went.

I have to be honest and say that I really did put a fair amount of effort into training myself mentally. I had not only read all of my mental training books weeks before but I also started thinking about them again the week of the race. In fact, while I was staying in Memphis the week prior to the race, I wrote a bunch of positive thoughts down on a piece of hotel paper that I was going to say to myself before and during the race. I carried it all week.

THE ALCOHOLIC IRONMAN

All week, I tried to visualize myself crossing the finish line. I kept playing the voice inside my head, "John Toth, you are an Ironman." The Rev3 had made me realize how important it was to stay positive the whole race, and that's what I decided to do. No matter what happened, no matter what the circumstances, I was going to stay positive and enjoy the day. I was going to smile and have fun and enjoy this once-in-a-lifetime opportunity.

The swim start was exactly as it had been described to me, a blender. There were three thousand people, all essentially trying to get into a single-file line in the water. After all, the fastest way to move when doing a lap is in the inside lane. The people that go on the outside end up swimming twice as far.

In some ways, it wasn't as bad as I had expected; in others, it was worse. I had heard that there could be punching and kicking and knocking people's goggles off. I didn't really have that. I just had people. People everywhere. Every stroke I took, I hit someone. Every kick I kicked, I hit someone. It was absolutely as crazy as everyone said. And I loved every minute of it.

I was a bit concerned for about the first ten minutes. That concern was more of me wondering if it would ever thin out. If you can't use your full stroke and are just kind of battling along, the race will be longer.

After the ten minutes, it did thin out a bit. That's when I really started to enjoy it. I was able to swim with the wetsuit on with no problem. I could breathe fine and was doing well. When it finally started to thin out, I started to actually look at it like a NASCAR race. I could see people in front of me who I wanted to pass. There were times that I got cut off and had to hit the brakes. There were times that I needed to pit stop and clean my goggles. It was awesome.

I swam the entire 2.4 miles in 1:22.

Holy crap! 1:22!

My first sprint took me almost forty-five minutes, and that was half a mile. I just swam my first Ironman swim, 2.4 miles, all because I didn't give up after my first triathlon swim. That was powerful to me. You would think that something like that would hit you later upon reflection. Not me. I wasn't even out of the water, and I was smiling. I did it. I just completed a swim at an Ironman.

When I got out of the water, I took my time as usual. The nice thing about something like the Ironman is that they have wetsuit strippers there when you get out of the water. What that means is that you just lay on your back and two guys rip the wetsuit off of you. It takes them three seconds. If you were to do it by yourself, it could take you three minutes.

After I got my wetsuit off, I started walking the quarter mile to transition. I made it a short bit when I realized that I could run. I actually still had some energy after the swim. Imagine that.

I got to transition and got all my stuff together. I made sure I put sunscreen on and then my bike shoes, sunglasses, and helmet.

Probably one of my proudest moments during the race was when I was leaving transition with my bike; I was leaving with everybody else. In almost every race I had been in to date, I had left transition alone. By the time I had gotten out of the water, 75 percent of the bikes were gone. Not today. Today I was right in the mix. It felt awesome!

One of the things that I hadn't noticed during the swim was the fact that it had started raining. I think if it had been a lot of rain, I may have noticed, but during the swim, it was only a light drizzle.

That changed about three minutes after I got on the bike, when a torrential downpour began.

I wasn't actually that upset that it was raining as much as I was curious if it would last all day. I hadn't really prepared for it to be cold. It was the end of July, and it was a perfect temperature. But when you are wet, it changes everything. I had a long-sleeve jacket in my special needs bag for the run, but I wasn't going to see that for fifty-six more miles.

The rain came down in buckets, and I kept riding. If a negative thought came into my head, I knocked it out with something positive. I would learn to repeat this a hundred times per mile on the bike.

The only bad thing about the rain was the danger that it brought. Lake Placid is a fairly hilly course, so much so that I was greatly concerned about it after my disaster at the Rev3. I had gone on some forums and gotten some positive feedback, so I felt a little bit better.

The upside to hills is that they come down, too. There was a fairly large, long hill at the beginning of the bike. It had been raining cats and dogs the whole way up. When I got to the other side, we started down. At the point when I finally hit the brakes going down, I was doing thirty-seven miles per hour. Thirty-seven might not sound like that much in a car; on a bike, it is flying! On a bike in the rain, it was suicidal.

I would have been scared if the road were completely dry. It wasn't, and I knew that. One little pebble, one little slip, and not only was I out of the race, I would have been taken out in a helicopter.

Having learned some humility in sobriety and determined to enjoy myself, I simply hit the brakes a little. I was still probably doing 27-30 miles per hour, but I was in control. Problem, solution.

Luckily, it only rained for about fifteen minutes. After that, it was an absolutely perfect day. A lot of my prayers must have been answered.

The first lap of the bike course was great. I can't imagine a more beautiful race venue. Every turn had a new stream and a new set of mountains to look at. If you weren't careful, you could end up crashing because you spent so much time looking at the beauty.

We were on the second hill after the rain had stopped. I didn't want to hammer my legs, so I just took my time.

A guy rolled up next to me and said, "Take your time. It's only lap one; you're doing great."

I thanked him and he said, "There are a lot of first-lap heroes in this race; you'll see. Take your time, and pace yourself."

That was great. That was some positive reinforcement that I could use. Take your time and don't kill yourself and everything will be okay. That's just what I did.

There were parts of the race that were long and flat, and you could fly. Then there were the hills. The hills were hills. But they weren't anything that I couldn't handle. Some of them I put my head down on, and some of them I talked with someone the whole way up. I met a guy doing his residency at NYU, and we talked about the world cup for twenty minutes. The next thing I knew, we were at the top of the hill.

Later, I had met a guy that lived about twenty minutes from me. We rode together for fifteen miles. He was from Doylestown, Pennsylvania. I am from Fort Washington. That's one of the coolest things about the Ironman and triathlon as a whole. It is a very welcoming and encouraging community of people. You can be half a race behind someone, but when you pass each other going in opposite directions, most people will shout words of encouragement to you. It is really one of the things that make this sport unique. If you need help, just ask. If you need encouragement, it's there for you. If you want company, it's all around.

The first bike loop was fairly uneventful, with the exception of the last twelve miles. While nothing big happened, for the most part, the entire twelve miles was uphill. Believe it or not, it's not as bad as it sounds; it's not Mt. Everest. It's just long and up, and you never get a break.

Even though the hills were tough, I made it back to transition still upbeat. Had there not been hills at the end, I actually would have had a pretty fast time. But there were hills, and now I know I need to work more on hills.

When I got back to special needs, the volunteers again were awesome. I gave them my race number, 1082, and they went and found my bag. I reloaded all of my water bottles and then pulled over to use the restroom. I wouldn't normally do that, but seventeen hours is a long time to go without using the toilet.

It's funny how your mind can play tricks on you. On lap two, I remembered some of the easy parts as being easier and some of the hard parts as being harder. There were spots where I was expecting a break and got none and others where the hill wasn't as bad as I thought.

All in all, I felt fine on the bike. What most people think is that it's your butt that hurts. That may be true for some people. (Not me; I have an Adamo saddle, which has the middle cut out so your nether region doesn't go numb). It's everything else. It's your wrists from holding onto the bike for seven plus hours; it's your lower back; it's your neck. It's really everything. Your butt and your legs are actually the things that bother you the least. You're just tired of being on the bike.

While my legs and my butt were okay, I was absolutely ready to get off the bike. Every part of me wanted off of that bike as fast as I could. Imagine sitting with a fence between your legs for six hours. It's just a long time to be sitting in one position. Even with all of the positive thoughts in my head, I was still ready to get off the bike.

When I finally got to the top of the final twelve-mile hill, I was ecstatic. I had been wearing a watch the entire time and knew right where I was. When I finally crossed the timing mat with my bike, I had covered 112 miles in seven hours and twenty-nine minutes, not great but not horrible. For a first time 205-pound man to ride 112 miles after swimming 2.4 miles, I was thrilled.

What I was even happier about was that I finished the first two legs of the race in nine hours. That gave me eight hours to complete the marathon. While I had been calculating this the whole time I was on the bike, when it was official, I couldn't help but smile. Despite the aches and pains, I knew I had a shot at being an Ironman.

I got into transition and gave my bike to a volunteer. I got all of my stuff and headed for the run tent to put on my gear. Boy, did it feel good to be off that bike!

I slathered myself with round two of suntan lotion and was out the door. I had decided early on that I was going to have fun and enjoy the race and now that I knew I had eight hours to complete the marathon, this was my chance.

If you have never been to an Ironman before, it's kind of like a rock concert. There are people everywhere. But unlike other races, it continues for almost the whole run. That's thirteen miles of spectators. It's like a giant tailgate party. There is music blaring and people with kegs on their front lawns. Some people have dinner parties, and others just come out to cheer. There are very few parts on the course where there isn't someone there cheering at you. It's kind of funny when I think about it. A few years before I would have been one of the people sitting on my front lawn with a keg behaving like a lunatic. Now here I was, actually doing the race.

Knowing that I had eight hours to complete the marathon and that I could probably walk it in six, I left transition with a big smile.

"If anyone wants a free tri-bike, mine is in row eighteen if you want it," I yelled as I exited transition.

The whole crowd laughed. About ten other people doing the race all agreed. We were all tired of being on the bike.

I managed to run for the first couple of miles. My goal was to run until I got tired, and then walk a little. Repeat, repeat, repeat. And that's what I did.

I spent six hours making friends and high fiving spectators. I saw my buddy from the Doylestown and yelled, "Hey, Doylestown."

He responded, "Hey, Fort Washington." We probably did that six times as we kept passing each other.

I met a guy from Washington, DC, who was doing his first Ironman and spent a few miles with him. He called me, "Philadelphia." I met a woman from Boston doing her second. She didn't finish her first. I met another guy from Doylestown and spent a few miles with him.

This went on and on for hours.

About ten miles into the marathon, I was starting to lose my energy. I hadn't actually eaten anything solid in over ten hours. While my plan was to stick with the liquids that I bought, I needed something in my stomach.

One of the interesting things at an Ironman is the things that they have at the aid stations. Aid stations on the bike are spaced out every eight miles. They have them every mile on the run.

The menu usually includes:

- Water
- Some form of sports drink
- Gels
- Oranges and bananas
- Pretzels
- Cookies
- Flat Coca Cola
- Chicken Broth

The last four are the ones that always got me. That is until I did an Ironman. You would think that all of these healthy people wouldn't eat any of these. Not even close. There is something about cookies that just make you feel better when you are out of gas. I don't know if it was the calories or the sugar, but they sure do, same with the pretzels. The flat Coke I had read about but wasn't a believer until I had some after mile thirteen. It's the elixir of life at an Ironman. I don't know how to explain it; it just is. And chicken broth—getting something warm and nutritious inside of you is always good.

The first thing I grabbed were cookies. Eating a cookie after ten hours of exercise is heaven. I knew that I couldn't feast, so I came up with a plan. I would eat a little bit at every aid station. I would also drink a small cup of water and a small cup of Ironman sports drink.

I followed this plan religiously for the next six to eight miles. I was going completely by how I felt. Although I came in with a plan, it was just as important for me to adjust as I went. I had stuck with bad plans too many times before.

As the miles went on, I ate less and less. I didn't need to fuel as much and didn't want to get full. By mile twenty, I was on a straight liquid diet again and feeling good. My legs were tired, but I knew I was going to make it.

It was just about mile twenty when I hooked up with Chip again. Chip was the second guy I had met from Doylestown. He and I had also traded passes a few times. Now we were together. Chip and I spent the last hour of the race getting to know each other, much like Frank and I used each other to keep our minds occupied during Rev3, Chip and I did the same thing during the last six miles of the Ironman.

We shared training stories and talked about people we both knew. We talked about which races we had done and enjoyed looking at the people having dinner parties on their front lawn.

I was still enjoying every part of the run. Even though I was tired and my feet were killing me, I was still having fun. When I passed the Ford girls who were dancing and blaring AC/DC, I pumped my fist in the air. When I ran past Elvis (who was doing the race), I yelled! Every single time, he yelled back, "Thank you, baby," in his best Elvis voice. He could barely make it up a hill but still did the voice; it was hilarious. When I ran past the girl with the "Free Hugs" T-shirt, I ran up and gave her a hug. It took me eleven months of training and almost twenty years of drinking to get here. I wasn't going to miss any of it.

Chip and I passed the time like two old buddies. When we got back to the general area of the start/finish line, I knew I was going to be an Ironman. I was tired, but I was putting one foot in front of the other.

At this point, we were walking. What was funny was that we were walking so fast, we were actually passing some people who were running. Realistically, they were doing the "Ironman Shuffle," not really running. It's what a lot of people do at the end when they are out of gas just to keep themselves moving forward.

We chatted away the last two miles. When we were about four or five hundred yards from the finish, he said to me, "Are you going to run in?"

I said, "Hell yes!"

Just when I started to run, I looked up and saw my wife. She yelled something, and then I heard her yell to the kids. I saw the whole family right before I crossed the finish line. I waved and kept going with the finish line within earshot.

I really thought that I would get emotional coming into the finish. I had actually gotten emotional a few times in the days before. I thought that all of the training and all of the sacrifice would come pouring out of my eyes when I crossed the line. As it was, I didn't. I don't think I had enough energy to be emotional.

As I made my way around the speed-skating oval, I could finally see the finish line. There were a thousand people or so in the stands. I felt like I was in the Olympics. It was awesome.

As I made my way to the finish line, I blocked out the thousands of screaming people and blaring music and heard only one thing, "John Toth, you are an Ironman!"

With that, I pumped my fist to myself and held it for a good five seconds and crossed the finish line.

I was an Ironman.

I turned around long enough to see Chip cross the finish line fifteen seconds behind me. He was greeted by his wife. We high fived and thanked each other for the company. Did I mention that Chip was sixty-five years old?

Going Home

After the race, I was cooked. I finished the run in 6:06, which put me a little over fifteen hours of constant movement. I had been moving so long, it actually felt weird to stop. A volunteer grabbed me and asked me if I was okay. I was. I had seen so many horror stories on television about people collapsing at the end of an Ironman that I almost expected it. But I was fine. I grabbed some water and my T-shirt and went to find the family.

Gabriella met me at the transition exit and took my bike. We weaved our way through the crowd and found Mom and Emily. I gave my wife a kiss and thanked her for all her support. She deposited me in front of the local courthouse so that I didn't have to walk the mile to go get the car.

I sat on the front step of that building, alone, thinking about the day. The year. I had just done an Ironman. I was first and foremost an alcoholic; now I was an Ironman, absolutely unbelievable. If you would have told me a few years ago that I could do something like this, I would have bet everything that I owned against it. Literally.

Once I realized that I had really done it, I texted my friend John and my dad. It simply said, "I did it. 15 hours"

When we got back to the hotel, I was okay physically but pretty tired. Chip had done a couple Ironmans before, so I asked him how much I was going to hurt the rest of the week, to which he said, "A lot."

I got myself situated and went to sleep with the weight of the entire world having been lifted off my shoulders. "I can't believe it; I did it." Smiling ear to ear.

The next day, I actually woke up first. My wife and the kids were sleeping, and I was already packing the car. Once they rose, we packed quickly and headed for home. Over the previous few days, I had gotten some messages from people that I knew wanting to see how I was doing and wishing me luck. Sitting in the car on the ride home, I sent the following message from my Blackberry:

> Good morning, I wanted to thank everyone for their well wishes for my Ironman this weekend. It was much appreciated.
>
> I started at 7am and finished just after 10pm. So it took me 15 hours to cover 140.6 miles. Which for a 6'3", 205 pound man, I will take. I actually don't feel too bad today with the exception of my feet. They feel like I walked across burning coals and then put them out with sandpaper.
>
> Anyway, I just wanted to say thanks to everybody and let you all know that I finished. I have one more email to write. I have a few words for Dick Hoyt!
>
> Thanks again!

Lessons Learned

The thing that has gone through my head over and over since I started this journey is the fact that I am a regular guy. There is nothing special about me or unique that allowed me to do this. Yes, being an alcoholic makes the story a bit more "Hollywood," but it doesn't help you get in the pool at 5:30 a.m.

Getting sober is one of the greatest things that ever happened to me. But getting sober didn't make me an Ironman. It allowed me to become an Ironman. There are a number of things that I learned in sobriety that I try to use in everyday life and tried to use throughout my training. I realized very early on in my training that my journey was going to be no different than the journey of life. There were going to be ups and downs. I would laugh and cry, but I had to keep going no matter what happened.

Part of the reason I wanted to write this book was to show other people considering recovery that they had other options in life. I thought when I first got sober that the whole world was going to end and I wouldn't have anything to do. I see it on the faces of new people when they try to get sober. They sit there trying to figure out why they would want to live sober. Being sober is so much more than simply not drinking. It's learning how to live life to its fullest.

The further along I got in my journey, the more I realized that what I was going through applied to more people than just alcoholics. I am a regular guy with a regular job and a regular family. I said it before, and I'll say it again, I wasn't a high school swimmer or track star. I am as regular as you can get with this stuff. I really am better suited to be a tight end or a hockey player than a triathlete.

I truly believe from the bottom of my soul that anyone can do something like this, no matter what it is. If you asked me that question five or six years ago, I wouldn't have believed you. My goal in writing this is to tell you that you can. You can do anything that you put your mind to, anything.

I didn't used to believe that. I thought that was just some saying that people came up with to make you feel better. It's not. I realize that if you are 4'1", you are not going to play center in the NBA. That's not what I'm talking about. What I'm talking about is something that you can achieve by working for it.

If you can put one foot in front of the other and do the work just like I did, you can accomplish anything you want.

Excuses are just that, excuses. It's sometimes easier to take the quick way out. A lot of times, we want things, but we don't want to do the work. That was me. I wanted to be a professional baseball player, but I didn't want to put in the effort. I wanted to just show up and be great. I wanted to be a famous musician but wanted it to happen for me without putting in the work. I wanted to be wealthy and expected to hit the lottery.

The truth is that you have to work for it. If you sit down with a goal and put your mind to it, you can do it. I did, and I am nobody special. Trust me.

> God grant me the serenity to accept the things I cannot change, courage to change the things I can, and the wisdom to know the difference.

Known as the serenity prayer, this little gem is one of the most powerful things I have ever learned. While it has been adopted by alcoholics around the world, it is not an alcoholic prayer.

In the process of getting sober, I have read my fair share of books, from the Bible to books on Buddhism to *The Art of Living* to the *Tao Te Ching*. It's amazing how much they all have in common.

One common theme I noticed early on in all of them is this simple philosophy: Let me learn how to accept things the way that they are. The idea being that we not waste our time and energy on things we have no control over. We probably all believe this concept, but it's difficult to practice in real life.

While it may sound odd, I used this all the time during my training. As you can probably already tell, I constantly worried about everything. What you probably didn't know was how many times I ran things through this little prayer. "Can I control this? Should I control this? Is there anything that I can do?"

Accepting the fact that I am a 205-pound man is simply the truth. Can I do anything about it? Maybe, to a degree. I could lose a few pounds. But will I ever be Craig Alexander? No. I accept that.

The courage to change. Do I have the ability to go from an overweight, drinking, smoking, 230-pound man to an Ironman? Yes. I can change the things that are in my control. I can focus my energy on something positive. I can ask questions and get help when I need it.

LESSON NUMBER TWO—I HAD TO GO THROUGH WHAT I NEEDED TO TO COMPLETE THIS RACE

I needed to go through every single race that I did to complete my Ironman. While that may not be true for everyone, it was for me. I don't know if it's because I am a slow learner or tried this without a coach, but I had to learn a lot of different things in a lot of different races to prepare me for the Ironman.

While this may actually sound somewhat deflating, it's simply how I managed to look at it. Sobriety had taught me to look at the negatives as learning experiences, and that's just what I did.

I almost drowned. I did my first race on a pogo-stick. I ate enough for a small village. Then I tried to drown again.

Each time I felt defeated, but each time, I got back up. I kept telling myself that these were simply learning experiences and that I couldn't give up.

Crossing that finish line proved that to me. In sobriety, we often say, "You have to go through what you have to go through to get here." That was the same for me in the Ironman. Having gone through what I went through made it all that much sweeter and made me all that much more grateful.

LESSON NUMBER THREE—PUT ONE FOOT IN FRONT OF THE OTHER

There were times in my training when I literally had to do just that. I put one foot out and followed it with the other. There were dozens of days that I simply didn't want to run. I told myself, "Just take the first step." There were days that I didn't want to do the Ironman anymore. So I decided to just do today's workout. I wasn't going to worry about the two hundred more workouts that I had to do, just today's. Sometimes, it's as simple as that.

I didn't just sign up and automatically want to do each workout each day. I struggled with my alcoholic brain the entire time.

I have a tendency to look at everything from a big-picture standpoint. When I don't want to work out, I think of how many of sessions that I have to do as a whole. I combine all of the workouts into one gigantic episode of grief for myself. The truth is that I only have to worry about today's workout, not tomorrow's or yesterday's, just today's. When I am having trouble getting off the couch, sometimes I just have to take the first step. It's almost always followed by another.

Lesson Number Four—Ask For Help, Then Ask Again

The night I got sober, I had met a couple of guys who had been sober for a long time. I remember it like it was yesterday. They sat across a table from me and told me all about themselves and how they used to be just like me. One of the things that they said stuck with me. "You don't have to do this alone."

I was awesome at quitting drinking; I did it all the time. It's staying quit that was hard for me.

One of the things that can happen in sobriety is that you can do it with other people. You make friends. You laugh together; you struggle together. When you need to complain about your boss, you call one of your sober friends. When you want to complain about your husband, you call one of your sober friends. If you want to drink, you call one of your sober friends.

The idea is that you are all going through the same thing. Sometimes you talk to someone who is going through the same thing; sometimes you talk to some who already did. What you don't want to do is sit at home on your couch, trying to figure it out by yourself.

This lesson in sobriety translated well for me when doing the Ironman. As I have said before, don't be afraid to ask for help. I have asked some of the most basic questions to people. You know what? They gave me an answer. You know why? Because at some point, they didn't know either.

If you are too proud or too macho to ask for help, I feel bad for you. There are tons of people out there who are willing to help. With today's technology, there are websites everywhere. Don't just sit there in your own head and try to figure it out. Ask for help! That's what I did.

LESSON NUMBER FIVE—"SEVENTY PERCENT AND COURSE CORRECT INSTEAD OF 100 PERCENT TOO LATE"

That quote is from an author named Donovan Campbell, who wrote the *New York Times* bestseller *Joker One*. Donovan was a Princeton University graduate and a marine who served in Iraq and Afghanistan. I had the pleasure of hearing him speak at a sales conference last year.

One of the things that he said stuck with me. Being a marine in Iraq, he was constantly in a hostile environment. Creating strategies, he did not have the luxury of a board room or a projector. They often had to make decisions about marines' lives in seconds. He said what the Marines had taught him was that it was better to have 70 percent of a plan and adjust as you go than to have a 100 percent correct plan after everyone was already dead.

I have probably said that about a thousand times at my job this year. Perfect plans and perfect ideas are not always necessary. Me signing up for the Ironman was 70 percent. I had an idea what I would do but had to figure out the rest along the way.

There were times where I locked myself into the 100 percent side of things, and it was actually worse. I was so focused on training that I didn't give myself any margin for error. You get tired, physically and emotionally. You need to have the flexibility to adjust as roadblocks come up. Not only do you need to be able to adjust, you also need to be able to do it and not feel wrong or guilty about it.

It's life. Kids have soccer games and holidays come up. You can't be so rigid that everything around you suffers. It will actually help you to be 70 percent. You can course correct as needed.

LESSON NUMBER SIX—IT'S THE CLIMB

I can't believe I'm actually going to quote Miley Cyrus in my book. But it's true. It's the climb; where you find out the most about yourself is climbing, not finishing.

While finishing a race is absolutely one of the greatest feelings in the world, what makes it great is what you had to go through to get there. Don't discount that. If you could just walk up and do a race like that, it wouldn't mean as much.

The mental challenge is, hands down, the hardest part.

I spent so much time with myself during training. I really learned things about myself that I just didn't know before.

Staring at the black line at the bottom of the pool for five hours a week with no iPod is hard. But you figure out how to deal with it.

Running for two hours the day after you rode seventy-five miles on your bike is daunting. You figure it out.

Sitting on a bike in front of your TV for five hours because it is raining so hard you can't go outside is miserable. You figure it out.

There are literally thousands and thousands of little challenges and little mental victories that you have to go through. I would sit and ponder how miserable I felt about having to ride my bike for five hours on Saturday. Then when I was actually on the bike, I realized that the thought of it was worse than the actual ride.

Life is a lot like this. If you were always at the top, the only way to go is down. What makes you a better person and defines who you are is what you do while you're climbing up the mountain.

LESSON NUMBER SEVEN—KEEP QUITTING AND THEN KEEP STARTING OVER AGAIN

I've said a lot of times that this is mental, and if you didn't hear me, *this is mental!*

If you are like me, sometimes you just need to get things off your chest. That's normal.

When I first started this training, I was extremely rigid and extremely disciplined. If I even thought about wanting to quit or give up, I would mentally beat myself up unmercifully.

It took me a while to learn, but sometimes, you just need to get it out of your system. Just like it sometimes feels awesome to scream at the top of your lungs in your car. Sometimes you need to release the tension.

Your whole body can become like a giant bottle of champagne that you keep shaking. You put more and more pressure on yourself and have no release. You need a release.

So quit. Yell at the top of your lungs how much you hate training. Tell your spouse that you want to sell your bike. Tell your kids to get you an extra large sundae with all the trimmings.

Now, start again.

I know this might sound stupid, but try it. You are going to want to quit something like this. What I am saying is to let yourself. Let your body purge all of the negative thoughts. Remind yourself of what it feels like to not have the weight on your shoulders. Remember what it is like to breathe.

After you relax for an hour or so, you'll quickly realize that you don't want to quit. You have to keep going.

Don't force yourself not to quit; force yourself to keep going after you quit.

LESSON NUMBER EIGHT—HAVE A REASON

For me, it has been important when trying to accomplish something to have a reason. Without one, it can be difficult for me to keep focused or remember why I started the journey.

In a case such as the Ironman, where you are training for half a year, it can be easy to quickly forget why you are doing this to yourself. Why do I really need to get up at 5:30 a.m.?

Think about how many diets you have started. How many have you quit? How many things in your life did you really want to do but didn't have a good enough reason?

I realized this fact when I was in my early twenties. I was drinking a lot and eating anything that I wanted. I had seen a picture of myself and couldn't believe how fat I looked. I was probably thirty pounds overweight. I quickly joined the gym. I lost all of the weight in less than four months. Why was I successful when thousands of people in the world can't make it a week at the gym?

My answer, I had a reason. What was my reason? Girls.

The honest answer is that I was in my early twenties and wanted to find a girlfriend/wife. If I was going to show up at the bar with my stomach hanging over my belt, what kind of girl was I going to get? That's how I looked at it.

While that may be a silly reason to some people, it was my reason, and it worked for me. When I didn't want to go to the gym, I thought about all of the girls that wouldn't talk to me. If I wanted to eat a cheesesteak every day, I thought about all of the girls that wouldn't want to talk to me. I had a specific picture in my head and wanted it bad enough that I would have done anything to get it. I had a reason.

Whatever your reason, you have to have one. You have to have something to fall back on when your simple "want" for something fades. Your reason can be as simple or as complex as you want.

My reason for doing the Ironman started with myself and not being able to make it a lap around the track. It ended up being a metaphor for my sobriety.

Find yourself a reason, and you will find a reason to finish.

LESSON NUMBER NINE—
COMPARE YOURSELF TO YOURSELF

It's funny how much of a student of psychology I have become over the years. In all honesty, I used to think a lot of that stuff was a load of bull.

But as you get older and a bit more mature, you start to look at things a little differently.

While many people may have learned some of these things earlier in their lives, I apparently was a slow learner. Maybe because I was pickled half the time.

One of the things that we often talk about in sobriety is comparing yourself to yourself. What that essentially means is that we shouldn't compare ourselves to other people; we should compare ourselves to our own journey in life. Are we growing? Are we moving forward in a positive way?

Too many times, I hear people who are envious of other people. One of the things that I learned in sobriety is not to judge a book by its cover. While we drunks didn't invent that saying, boy is it true. You can look at someone who dresses right and says the right things, only to find out that they are completely crazy. How many times have you seen the rich, stay-at-home mom who puts on the act in public? Do you really think she is that happy?

The point is to compare yourself to yourself. You don't know what's going on with other people. You don't know what going on in their head in their lives. You may see someone who is swimming twice as fast as you. They may have been a competitive swimmer in college. You may see someone who looks happy all the time but is actually really depressed inside.

If you were to sit down and hear me play the guitar, you would say, "Wow, that's awesome, I wish I could play like that." If I didn't tell you that I have been playing for thirty years, you would think that I had some special trick. The truth is that I have been playing for thirty years; that's why.

Everyone is facing their own demons, even if you can't see it. If you see someone who seems to have the perfect life, chances are they don't. You don't need to, either. Enjoy the one that you have.

LESSON NUMBER TEN—COUNT YOUR BLESSINGS

If there is one thing that sobriety has taught me above all other things, it's to count my blessings.

It's funny to actually use that phrase. I don't remember if it was my grandmother or my mom who used to say that, but they said it often.

Before I got sober, I don't know that I appreciated anything. I often said that I did, but it didn't really have the same magnitude that it has now.

Being free from the fog of alcohol was the first step. The second step was to look around me and open my eyes. I have everything that I have ever wanted, a great wife, great kids, a home, a job that pays my rent, a good family, and a good head on my shoulders. Sometimes, it's a matter of opening your eyes.

I can say from the bottom of my heart that I am grateful for the life that I have today.

All I did was an Ironman. There are thousands of people in the world who lift much heavier burdens than I do. Look at people like Dick Hoyt. Look at my cousin Joe and his son. Look at the soldiers who die for us overseas without thanks. Look at the police officers who put their lives on the line every day to help us.

My dad has a saying that always puts things into perspective for me. "You think you have it tough, go spend the day down at Children's Hospital; then we'll talk about how bad you have it."

He's right. I am more grateful now than ever before. I'm grateful for the good times, as well as the bad. While I don't always like the bad, they make the good that much better.

Contact Information

John Toth can be reached at alcoholicironman@gmail.com and at his website, www.alcoholicironman.com.

Lightning Source UK Ltd.
Milton Keynes UK
UKOW06f1808221115

263306UK00004B/100/P

9 781613 461471